The *fire* of Prometheus

Poems of Transformation
By John Kuzma

With thanks to my wife Bess, whose patience, love, and support are known only to God, I dedicate this effort as we look forward to marking 50 years of marriage on June 29, 2018.

I wish to thank my excellent production team: Business Coach, Simon Zryd; Audio Recording, Taylor Marvin; Web Designer, Audra Brehm; Creative/Technical book design, Randi Daniels; Printing, OneTouchPoint; Photography, John Goerner, Non-Stop Productions; Marian Brenton, Augean Stables photograph; Mark Stalker, spiderweb photograph; Literary consultant, Kathy DeGette; Legal counsel, Jon Sutterlin; Computer technician, Dean Ingram; and Author's bio, Jean Sibley.

And finally, I wish to credit my psychological Comrade in arms in this heroic effort, Jack.

Yes, Jack, with me from the beginning, and knowing me better than any demon or angel that I know so well, and which tirelessly taunt me in black face or holy raiment. Yes, Jack is that most deeply human part of me: flawed to his core.

Indeed, but radiating love, as close to pure being as I shall ever know in this life.

Hard Jack's life wrung out him whose Archangel warrior ways writ hard lines of experience so's that Jack's formal, farewell photo looked a stranger at Jack's puzzling, and beckoned him to get up again, put on his shield and buckler, the only armor he ever had: the armor of light.

Too much star time encreased deep wagon tracks birthed his furrowed brow; too impressed by his own weltschmerz, his natural buns of steel and soft heart was Jack again: Sitzfleisch three times a day - - -

"Am that for keeps, Cosmo?"
August 2017

©2017 John Kuzma Music, LLC

About the Author

Words evoke images, and nowhere is that more evident than in John Kuzma's poetry.   John has written poetry his entire life, threading it into and around his life experiences. He spent his years working as a music educator, composer, organist, conductor, and philosopher, and is an avid scholar of Greek and Latin classics.

Born in Cincinnati, Ohio, John studied at the Cincinnati College-Conservatory of Music, and earned degrees from the Eastman School of Music and the University of Illinois. He was also the recipient of a Fulbright Scholarship to study organ in Copenhagen, Denmark.

John moved west to San Diego, CA, where he took his first church organ position, as well as teaching at San Diego State University and UC Santa Barbara. In 1980, he formed the San Diego Chamber Orchestra, and was a staff musical arranger at the Crystal Cathedral. He became the music director of the American Boychoir in Princeton, NJ, before moving to Denver, CO, to become the Minister of Music at Montview Boulevard Presbyterian Church, a post he held for nearly three decades. During his career, John conducted for various American regional orchestras, and has conducted in Europe, Canada, and Iceland.

John had successful Deep Brain Stimulation surgery for Parkinson's Disease in 2016-2017.

His many varied experiences, his love of words, and his keen observational powers have provided ample fodder for his poetry. John and his wife, Bess, live in Denver, Colorado, with cats Claude and Camille.

Writer's Bio by Jean Sibley

Contents

The Fire of Prometheus 1
Christmas Delivery 2
Jimmy's News 5
Leyden & Colfax 6
Bang 7
Friday Afternoon at the Bank 8
Purity 9
Supermarket 10
"Would you like to sign this petition?" 12
Supermarket - Cigar Head 13
Heaven and Earth in Little Space 14
My Real Destination 15
Moth 16
The Sage of Kearney Street 19
One Heck of a Dog 20
Mentorship 21
Thoughts on a Snowy Night 22
Sonnet of Confession 23
Cardiac Catheterization 24
Souls on the Stable Road 26
An Idea of Winter 27
Spider in the Cold 28
Snowy Last Night 29
What Do We Have, Really? 30
Augean Stables 31
Upon Waking During Deep Brain Stimulation Surgery . . 32
"Eskimo Pies"™ 34
Jungian Dream 35
A Bird Spoke to Me Last Night 36
Stravinsky's Sacre du Printemps at 100 37
My Room 38
Family 39
My Heart Dances Her Way – CardioDance 1 & 2 40
The Chronicle of Change 42
Thoughts Rambling on Monday Night 43
Transition to Final Things 44
Surfaces 45
Claude's Software of the Soul 46

Pygmies 47
What Isn't Obvious at the Buffalo Grill. 48
Prostate Trouble 50
Dream Song for Uncle Bill Kuzma 52
Ancient Warriors' Song 53
Unbearable Nostalgia 54
Jack Mad with Music 55
Afraid at Night 56
Committee Meeting 57
The Thing Itself I'll Be 58
Faust's Seeker 59
The Mirror 61
Ubiquitous Genius 62
Pate of Foie Gras 63
Scents 64
Auntie 65
Jack's Catenary Curve 67
Ιεροσόλυμα 68
The Fly 69
Solitude and Friendship 70
Organ Music at Cincinnati's "Old Odeon" 71
Hard 72
Composers' Panel 73
From Cosmo 74
A Monk of the Abbey 75
Rolodex™ 76
Ecclesiad 77
My Javelin 78
Ragtime 79
If I Don't Make it Home… 80
Faith Journey of a Catholic Child 81
Ordinary Gallantry 82
My Father's Funeral 84
Choir Rehearsal 86
Pondering My Finitude at 70 88
Genesis 22:13 89

A key to understanding these poems.

The Fire of Prometheus is a metaphysical construct, anchored in the psyche of every human being. To the criminal or the con-man it is the "last score" and quickly evaporates into merely the next score. To the wise, however, it is the fire of usefulness, a way of looking at things, a life attitude, a way around ego-centrism.

Prometheus stole fire from Zeus so that mankind could have it. His eternal punishment was to be bound to a rock and have his liver eaten each day by Zeus in the form of an eagle. But the damage was done: mankind had fire, for better or worse.

I believe that the possession of fire represents the dawn of consciousness. These poems, honestly recollected, are my account of ordinary people given the opportunity to use the fire of Prometheus either wisely or poorly.

The Fire of Prometheus

And I have grown my own version of courtly manners:

yes, grown

like a secret Bonsai in the dark, without the help of culture;
Grown with seeds

I stole from the overseers. And I learned to make fire also
alone in the darkness;

illumination came to me in these days, against my will,

by the awful grace of God.

Christmas Delivery

I walk in the morning chill
downhill on Champa Street,
the symphony librarian waiting for me in warmth
of backstage musicians' talk
and my envelope of orchestra parts for my new piece
tucked underarm, and warm beside me.

I pass a man sleeping there
on the pavement, his face childlike
in swaddles of gritty corduroy coat.
And two discarded bottles nearby
that were full of much that seemed important
just hours in the night ago.

I pass,
yes, pass by much more than all that, errand in mind,
delivery ahead.

I imagine more than I could see,
thinking of failed promise

walked past, slept through,
seen through an emptied bottle.

The musicians all know me by now,
through many years'
notes of mine they've played inside walls there,
downtown.

We say our "happy holidays," and it's uphill
all the way back.
Back past the discarded things I'd passed before:
the bottles, rags, and then,
I saw he'd turned over,
showing his amputated leg to the cold morning sun.

And city smells filled that morning air
as we rustled and stirred like stable boys
about important business and the music of the dawn.

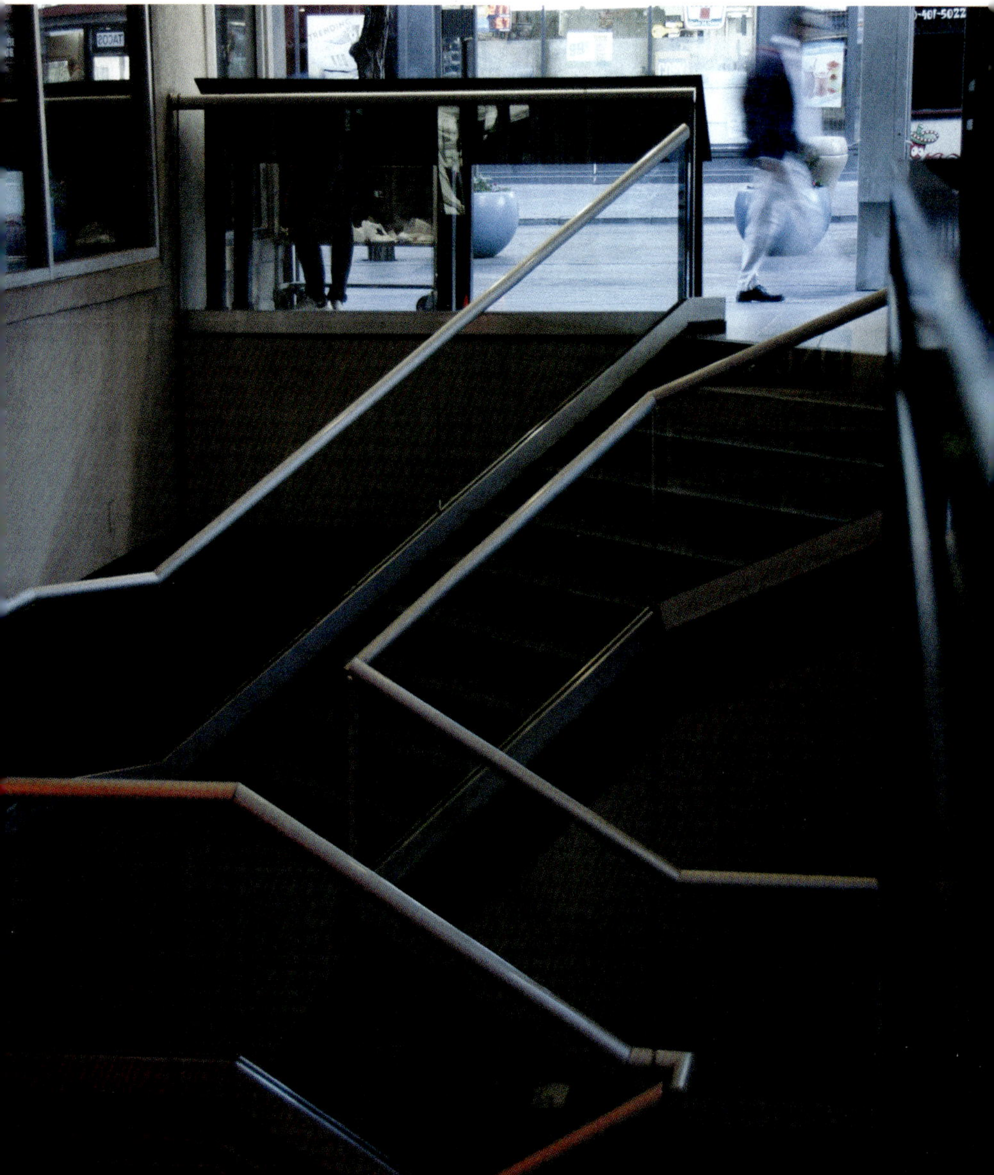

Jimmy's News

sits
below street level
on Champa St.
just off the mall,
and Jimmy
sits
behind his small counter.

Always smoking, he
practices guitar between customers
and fulminates generally
on all topics,
sage-like,
there in the basement.

I suppose six or eight businesses
have failed
in the larger,
adjoining basement space but
Jimmy prevails still.
In my memory,
it's been a dozen years.

He'd saved a certain magazine for me
when I called about a Tuesday Times.
No one in Denver but Jimmy
seemed to have the magazine
or the Tuesday Times.

Jimmy weighs in -

*"Sons of bitches shorted us, man;
shorted all of Denver by 1000 copies.
Son of a bitch.*

Told us they were printing in Phoenix now.

Told us this shit wouldn't happen any more.

Steamboat mouth and rowboat ass, I say.

This really bites my crank, man.

*I got my usual six copies
but they're all promised.*

*Here, want to read the Science section?
That's why you buy on Tuesday, right?*

Steamboat mouth and rowboat ass.

This really bites my crank."

I pay for my magazine,

"hey, you get the W/M discount."

What?

"White man's discount."

---

*Note to Jimmy from John:
  It's time to review your discount policy. Give me a call.

Leyden & Colfax

I never turn into the intersection of Leyden and Colfax
especially on a Saturday.

The supermarket there crowds me with yahoos
and all humanity battles at the entrance
there at Leyden and Colfax especially on Saturdays.

And today it is as always.
A minor league goddess drives I'd say 30 mph
through the fire lane,
such that I must trot a little to avoid her.

Outraged her stare,
white knuckles of brass,
barely seeing above the wheel,
she, molto in comitatu*
convenes court:

"Yo' ass is in d' fuckin' road"
"An' yo' ass is in d' fuckin' car," (and I didn't miss a beat).

There is a civilized man,
say, 70 or so,
wearing his Snap-on Tool™ windbreaker
so that I saw green
full in front of me as he shuffled by.

This ordinary Saturday unfolds
even now as I listen to a low double bass note
with gamelan in Lou Harrison's
Suite for Violin, Piano and Small Orchestra,
and I tell you here that future collisions
had best avoid me, when like now, I drive forward,
slowing here and there, as they do,
when I watch, and listen to silent eyes.

---

*molto in comitatu - "her great train in tow." From 1 Kings, Chapter 10, verse
  2, referring to the visit by the Queen of Sheba to King Solomon. The Latin
  comes from St. Jerome's Biblia Sacra Vulgata, 4th Century.

Bang

Booby-trapped 19, shot-gunned down, owner rigged.
The boy was looking for some tools to steal.

Blood pellets askew and home,
a glove to catch blood
dripping on a friend sought to revive.

Fixed a trip wire behind
which precious tools protected
It was the last of thefts for him, 19.

Wrenches I suppose live
greater than this pop-gun knows
an O, O totus floreo hills Arlington blow.

It was on the radio.
A vigilante in me listens,
I recall electrocution in New Jersey
by a private citizen, Fief: thief.

"That'll keep 'em awake,
but a guy can get in trouble doing that nowadays."

Friday Afternoon at the Bank

I smoke the last part of a small cigar,
at the bank, (back entrance).

Waiting for Bess to cash a school check
I spot two men.
One, driving a white cab, pulls up
within five feet of me, while the other approaches him,
unfurls a wad of many $100 bills whipping off twenty,
maybe thirty, and hands them (watching me)
into the cabbie's hands.

A new man,
"the spotter" appears,
to witness all this, me included.

The spotter:
a rock at 300 lbs., black cowboy boots
with brightly polished copper toes and heels.

His huge bottomed woman: black jeans,
boots to match his, follows him
after the transaction.

The spotter misses nothing. Will I be shot?

All have hands in pockets, like me.
The taxi driver hands back two of the hundreds,
with an apology, the other two
watch me through all this.

Then,
all depart: taxi man, payer,
miss huge bottom,
her spotter boyfriend.

All scan my presence
as I throw down my cigar in assent to what I'd seen.
All look squarely into my eyes.

The security guard comes out,
looks around.
I nod to him, meet Bess,
and walk away.

Purity

Deep in winter
fat young robins
chased by smaller flickers, lose their perch,
stunned.

At least a dozen drink at our pond.
Two fish,
white, yellow
hover, still.

The pond filled with winter cold
smells of decaying life.

Drunk full
they fly.
Spring ahead,
when will I see Winter again?

Supermarket

Tuesday morning about 6:30 is my usual
supermarket place and time,
I mind my own business,
ready for Advent and Christmas,
Pax in terra, not far off.

Two men in John Deere hats
 talk in the outside chill.
"They should'a dropped th'ay Bomb on
that Castro som' bitch 'long time ago."

A fair-skinned woman in tights,
wiry black hair askew,
picks up a penny, ponders,
then tosses it into the Thanksgiving
donation basket.

I feel better, and wonder
about this young ancient coin's journey.

I check my blood pressure there,
near the horse where you put a dime in
and ride awhile:
136/85. Not bad.

Now, *accel. agitato molto.*

A crazed, cross-eyed woman
charges me with her cart as I'm
distracted by a man,
all craggy and Rip Van Winkle,
especially his watery eyes.

Almost clear,
I'm too slow for a very dirty man
wearing a very wrinkled white shirt,
and very baggy shorts. He rushes my
right flank, moving fast,
maybe six inches from my butt.

Egad.

It seems I made him angry.
I swerve away, watch.
He mindlessly tromps on,
a spike-haired kid following dad's
diabolic tempo, a young indefatigable
nose picker, with much bluster
all his own.

I get my things, walk out,
find the car door, and drive.
Peaceful solitude beckons.

A pin-nosed woman,
all corn rows pulling at her skull,
starts chasing me in her shiny red car.

I turn to evade,
and an armed column of cars
is behind me as the light changes.
I turn onto a side street
and a small car pulls out from the curb
following close, real close.

There's no room
to pull over, no room
to let the lone stampeder pass.
He's now about five feet
from my bumper, edging closer
as if filling a vacuum
that sucks him forward.

I go faster, he hugs my rear.

What's with all this anyway?

11

"Would you like to sign this petition?"

On a bright summer day
I walk to the supermarket door
walking almost normally
for the first time six weeks after surgery.

My tendons were too short it seemed,
and while rejected as a soldier
I'd lived normally for many years,
even playing organ pedals
to my own astonishment at times.

Minding my own business
I approach,
on my own power,
without my walker,
my plaster cast off a few days.

A stranger approaches . . .

"Would you like to sign this petition?"

I recoil.

"No."

The concept seems simple enough,
and rejection seems even simpler.

"Why not?" he comes back at me.

"I don't have to tell you why not."

And this answer
required no practice, given as it was
on our own terms, seeming to me
honorable to us both.

"Are you an angry man?"
Well now, hostilities declared,

I enter into the world,
outside my entrenchment
that deceives me still now,
even since childhood.

"I don't have to answer that question either."

Now, rage emerges.

"What are you, a damned Fascist?"

And,
I didn't have to answer that either,
as we both knew.

Supermarket - Cigar Head

… was two places in front of me in the checkout line -
dark brown skin of his face and neck all Maduro tobacco.
And his close cut grey hair seemed, in proportion to his
body, like a hefty, nicely shaped cigar ash.

Fully lit with anger there in the line,
Cigar Head raged, raised hell,
fulminated over his pork sausage.

Now, I know the street smart checkout woman,
and she had sized up Cigar Head,
all grey headed herself.
She left us there knowingly nodding; left with alacrity.

She chased down his pork, anew.
Cigar Head muttered angry insults
to us in the line and to a few who passed
in via, about the store, raging about the state of things
in his Cigar Head.

My line partner (I'd say in her 80's, rail thin)
winked at me.

After about twenty minutes Cigar Head was "out the store"
on his muttering way.

Had he accomplished great things in his Cigar Head?

Heaven and Earth in Little Space

Bees, I am told,
make two million trips to individual
flowers to make a pound of honey.
And, they know how to customize the
hive to individual needs,
by shape and size.

Over the past few weeks
a pair of robins have built a nest
well out of any clever cat's reach
just under the garage gutter.

The male would bring his mate
a squirming worm,
or a flailing bug to eat
as she sat there, motionless,
looking at me as I passed.

Three fledglings finally appeared
moving head first upward,
mouths gaping
for whatever mom brought home.

Now,
I think of the weight of these creatures,
the birds an ounce or so,
the bees, what,
a pound for the whole hive?
And how do they know all this?
How much could a bird brain (the term
doesn't exist for nothing) weigh?

But being is in fact weightless.
A vine is one thing,
but a knot in a vine is quite another,
and adds no weight,
brings being into our Perseus mirror
obliquely, of course.
Is this the soul's weightless flight,
of pure being? And, effortlessly, do we
not carry God's own weightless genius
along with the birds and the bees?

The fledglings left today,
carrying timeless being,
weightless wisdom as they flew free.

My Real Destination . . .

. . . has been known to me since childhood.

And still, each day I set out for the new place.
I know so many
who travel to places I'll never see.
And as I age, more and more souls
my age have more and more time to travel.

Today I again saw travel ads in the newspaper,
with fares to so many places
and prices cheaper than ever.

Years ago,
performing on the road sometimes
over one hundred nights a year, it all seemed
a normal way to live.

Our bus would wind through city streets
lined with houses that seemed peaceful
as their gentle lawns and noble town halls.

But my real destination remained then, as now,
well known to me.

Abraham, we are told,
heard God's command to "go to a new place."

This is the meaning
of my true destination, as along each day's new path
I move about the ordinary places of my inner universe,
extraordinary in the abundance of the new.

Moth

A moth struggles on my desk.
Clearly damaged,
dying?

She flies straight at me
punching my cheek,
lands on the mousepad,
slowly taxies,
waits.

I ponder her,
fragile,
winged with symmetry
seen 100 million years ago.

I ease back,
find my magnifying glass,
and see her head
turn to look
into my eyes.

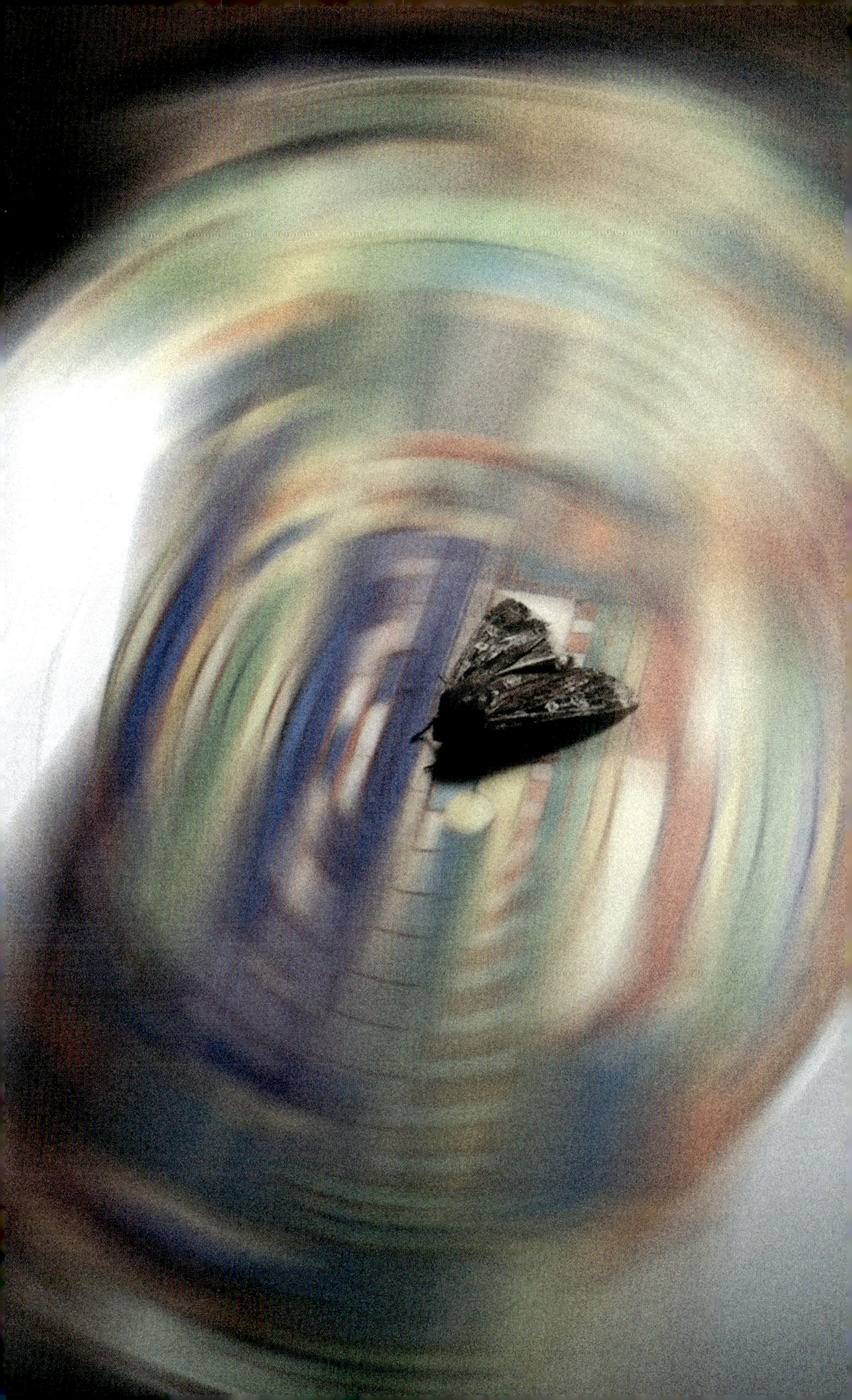

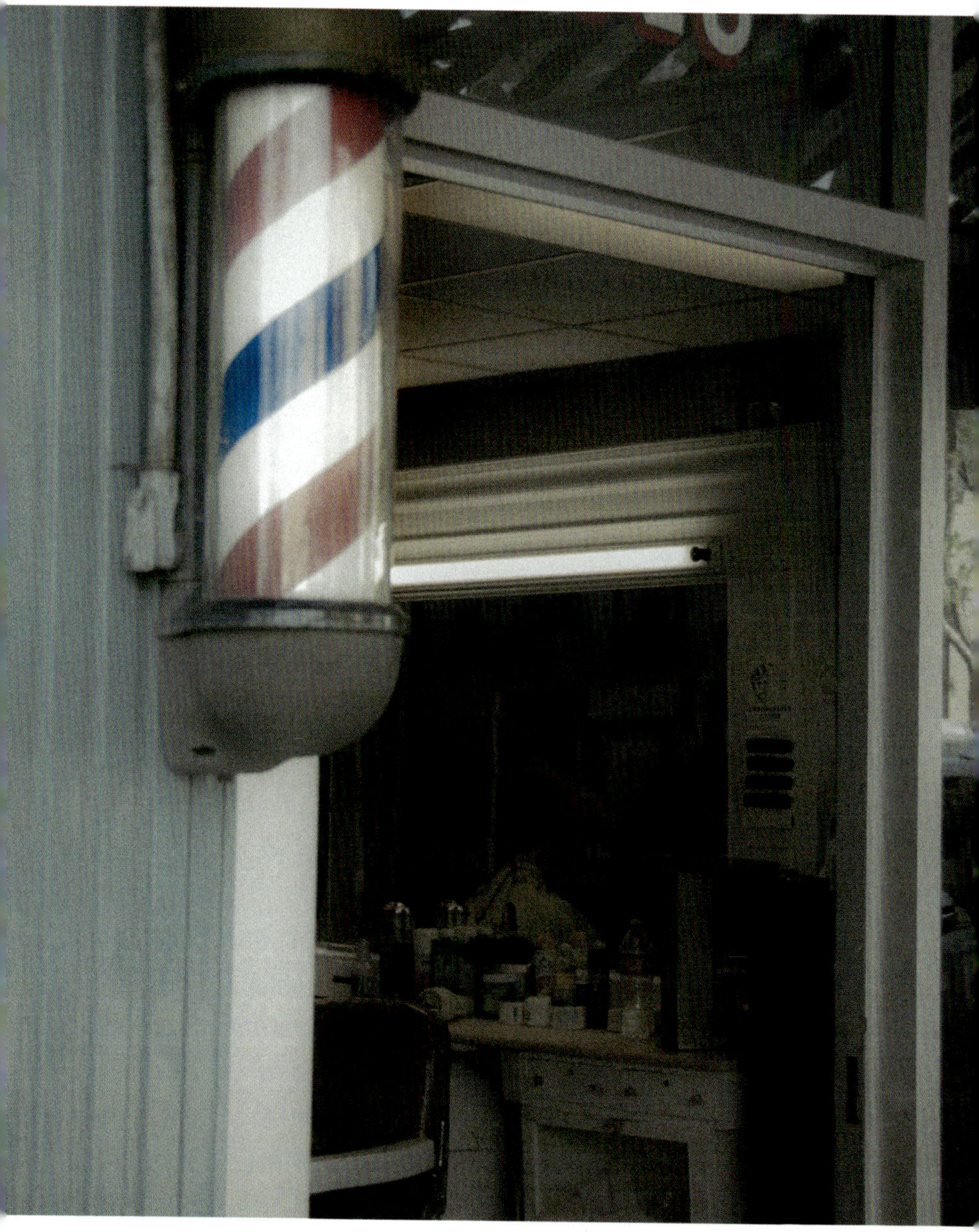

The Sage of Kearney Street ...

is a 57 year old African American man with whom I talk jazz,
African mythology, politics, Socrates,
Alexander the Great, the folly of humanity,
and all things. He is my barber, and my friend.

Paul Waterman presides at his shop
on Kearney St., near Colfax,
his shoulder length dreadlocks neatly braided.

"We have a multicultural shop here, John.
You can see by these posters here,
this one is Hispanic hair styles,
this here is African American,
and that one is Caucasian."

Paul sells incense, candy bars,
du rags, and various ointments and unguents.
The shop is immaculately clean.
In the men's room are pastel colored prints
of African American beauty salons,
peaceful scenes of peaceful lives.

A homicide detective for 25 years,
he learned to cut hair in the army.
"John, the criminal element is always with us.
It is our lower nature, which the Egyptians knew about.
And while we are in this physical form,
it will forever be with us."

Paul opens his shop at 6:30am
I appear around 7:00
and we sit and talk for a couple of hours.

He wants to return to Africa someday with his wife,
following DNA mapping of the huge African diaspora,
to his true ancestral nativity.

Paul has traced his lineage as far back
as American slave records go;
mostly bills of sale.

One Heck of a Dog

The dog appeared at our door,
a few nights before Christmas Eve.
Black with salt and pepper gray hair,
he was young and full of optimism
that seemed to proclaim
"I am one heck of a dog, you know."

Standing at about fifteen inches high
he fully expected us
to let him into the house,
set up his world headquarters here
forever, with us.

Bess called for my help
there at the side door.
He wouldn't have it,
being outside the house.

With a Solomonic tone I suggest
"Let's go to the front door,"
he follows,
tail wagging,
eager to come in that door, any door.

*"Our cats, Basil and Veronica,
would not have understood
his presence in the house,"*
I said (less Solomonic than before).

But, as he trotted away,
I wondered a bit
at how easily he put aside
disappointment:
his acceptance and trust
of another bright beginning
was without doubt.

The evening wore on.
Bess and I watched
the fire slowly grow dim.

It is time to check the doors;
time to call it a night.

Bess checks the front door,
calls to me: *"it's the dog again."*
Looking half frozen now
safely inside, we check his collar –
call the number on his tag.

His grateful owner returned our call
but only after about two hours had
passed, and *"Buddy"* had jumped into
bed with us, with our cats sequestered
in the bathroom.

Around 10:30pm,
Buddy was thrilled to see
his familiar family again.
Our happiness was muted only by
Buddy's tireless affection and comfort,
disarmingly given to us.

And as the evening's darkness took over
the night's frozen coldness,
thoughts of how the Christ energy,
always and everywhere,
appears at our door, and refuses denial.

Mentorship

Sarah is in third grade
and always in trouble.

Sarah is like Socrates,
Avila's Theresa, Aquinas,
and others who live the Way:
her sense of things,
usually misunderstood,
seems like a misguided magnet – a misaligned force.

And (except for one gifted teacher,
in tune with Sarah's psychic force field)
the wrong things are attracted and repelled.

Sarah was in trouble again, of course,
and her older mentor was there this time,
to help everyone sort through
the opposites flinging themselves into an abyss
too deep for most to ponder.

Hell itself seemed at the door,
with Sarah seeming Hell's next resident.

Her mentor spoke a few words,
walked on the waters,
calmed the tempest, for now.

"I want to go with you," the little girl said,
ready to drop her nets full of fish.

Now, we hear a drumbeat of cynicism,
flattering us with temptations
to seek the good in nothingness,
while the Christ energy beckons again,
at the darkest hour of night.

Thoughts on a Snowy Night

Denver's worst blizzard in many years
rages now, just outside our door.
Twenty-four inches of snow
would not be impossible.
The Interstate highways are closed
from downtown to the Nebraska and
New Mexico borders.

Stanley, one of my snow shovelers
left after half an hour's work early today.
Breathing heavily at 57, his
African genes are not built for this.

It was sunny, just yesterday,
and I played Mozart's K 545
for the funeral of a woman who
radiated light all around her.
None of today's cold intruded until,
well, as always with darkness, today.

Last Thursday the neighborhood fox
appeared at our front yard's gate,
fully furred in her red winter colors,
boldly confident, and then
walking with purpose
toward our back porch.

Does she live with her young under it?

Earlier this fall, on a cool day,
I saw our pond frog emerge
black and fat (I'd say 2 lbs.)
from, what, five years in the pond, now?

He confidently leaving us,
seeking his fortune.

I play Contrapunctus IV
from Bach's mighty Art of the Fugue,
in wonder at all life, now and then,
fueled by a divine child's life force larger
than us all.

Sonnet of Confession

Smooth Ray Charles' touch in "Georgia on my Mind"
(as grounded a full burden ever writ) informs me:
sky blue, heady memories: Muhammad Ali, Don King,
Howard Cosell, where are they now?

Evoking every bit
with deadly pip-sqweek bombs of every kind
like kids chase ice cream trucks past sentries blind:
I replaced the stolen mission bell.

I stole it thoughtlessly,
young man's oyster bought a passage counterfeit,
but real enough to fool the other fools
and roister all the temporary street creds' spiel
of pawning stolen missionary bells.

And thus did I escape the Devil's spells.

Cardiac Catheterization

Diana, all Apollonian, patrician and professional,
(my prep nurse): *"everything off, and don't tie the gown."*

Diana earns her pay with a painless IV,
left forearm top side,
as a tarty wench-like Jasmine does *"bedside check-in."*

Michael Jamison, physician's assistant,
looks like a young Warren Beatty
confidently briefs me,
then graciously disappears.

Within minutes, I'm gurneyed
into the brilliantly lit OR,
and meet my two excellent cardiologists:

Dr. Jeffrey Smithfield
and Dr. Stephen Mitchell.

Sedated with *"cardiac champagne"*
by Dr. Nick, my chubby anesthesiologist,
Dr. Smithfield makes a puncture wound
into my right femoral artery,
about 3 inches from my genitalia
into my right leg,
threads a tube through the aorta
and into the top of my heart.

An x-Ray machine 1" above my chest
shows all this to expert eyes.
Iodine dye pumped into my heart
instantly finds its way, illuminating every artery.

Egad,
90% blockage in one place
and 70% in another.
Within minutes these are dilated with a small balloon,
then held open by a small tube.

Full blood flow restored,
the puncture wound plugged with a man-made blood clot…
I am good to go with a new heart.
Beware the plug – *"Don't disturb this gizmo"*
I am warned.

"If it comes undone you could bleed to death in five minutes."

Dr. Mitchell: *"…there was just a thread-sized artery left."*
Consensus among the docs was that the stress of
my planned brain surgery almost certainly
would have led to a heart attack during surgery.

Afternoon slept through
led to friends' visits,
reflection on finitude,
the humbling art of music, my soul's voice.
I listen now in my treasured early morning solitude
to Elgar's Intro & Allegro,
full of life and full of confidence in the beautiful.

A boyish 69 in a few weeks,
I believe I'll be a boyish 99 in 2045
when my centennial year
will reckon hard on me my small contributions to humanity.

Musa dell'arte:
*"You've got work to do, John.
Let go of your Saturday morning blankets. Let's roll."*

Love, the muse, has again bade me welcome,
yet this time, my soul shall not draw back.

It is remarkable, isn't it?

Souls on the Stable Road

At a restaurant tonight
a group of three men came in,
and the youngest, maybe eighteen,
loudly stumbled on the single step to
the dining area.

I'd guess he was 90% blind.
His two companions didn't help him,
more out of respect
than any lack of caring for him.
Throughout the meal
I could see him in my eye's corner as he
struggled with simple eating tasks.

A few days earlier, in Cincinnati,
Sondra, a waitress at Price Hill Grill,
was alone, cooking,
waiting tables for, maybe, ten of us.
She answers the phone:
"hi honey, I love you.
Do you have your lunch money?
OK, don't forget to walk the dog after
school before I get home, I love you.
No, I'm here alone,
bye, I love you honey."

Lunch the next day at Price Hill Chili.
A deranged woman in from the cold,
spits and kicks at the floor.
Everyone seems to know her.
She sits in the booth behind me,
spitting and cursing furiously.
No one acknowledges her.

Mary, my waitress (maybe 65,
a veteran, chubby, tinted brown hair)
tells me: "honey, why don't you move
down here a few booths away from the
door where it's warmer."

There is a knowing wink, I stay, the wild
woman leaves in a few minutes.

I meet Eric's father,
a distinguished European man
whose gaze sizing me up
marks his keen intelligence
as much as his patrician bearing.
It would set him apart in any crowd
for one with a practiced eye.

His son, Eric, leases computers to me
when I need them.
And dad, well, dad developed some
early computer chip for NASA,
and today fixed his son's computers
like child's play.

Eric gives me a big intro, mentioning the
American Boychoir…

"Do you know the Regensburg Boychoir?"
the father asks.

"Sure, my guys almost beat them
in soccer once, and they can really sing.
They're called…"

…I ready my German accent but he
beats me, answering in English

"the Cathedral Sparrows. Isn't it
wonderful, this MIDI ?!…"

As I remember these souls tonight,
I imagine the all-embracing love that
our small effort engenders for us as
snow fills our tracks to the stable.

"If thou wilt foil thy foes with joy,
Then flit not from this heav'nly Boy."
–Robert Southwell 1561-1594

An Idea of Winter

There is an idea of Winter dark
that fills my inner space with life.

It has always been and remains
profound in me.

The darkening of days
adding up to weeks
creates industry in action and
incarnation through artifacts.
And *"Winter is icumen in"* rolls
through me in deep laughter.

Yes,
this will forever be my best of times.

As coldness numbs from the outside,
all pain subsides and hope seems
invincible.

In the kitchen, my new pressure cooker
silently works miracles here at altitude,
softening what went into it
impenetrable leaving all malleable
as my spirit
pressed about
by the gentle touch of a child.

Spider in the Cold

On December 30 at about 6:00pm a spider tries to climb the wall next to me.

She (I assume) is frail from the looks of repeated failed hoisting of her own small weight.

Outside, snow falls, and they say it will be -7 degrees tonight, so putting her outside is not an option.

Snowy Last Night

Snow last night and today. New shovelers,
along with a veteran, a bit crazy now,
labor on the sidewalks.

The dark drear of the present looms large.
No going out on this night before Christmas Eve,
as frailties of age muster forces who knows how large?

Others, high and low, have crossed these Alps of doubt.
Hannibal lost what, 30,000 men,
forty elephants
and what not of his soul, counted except by God?

A cold night teaches big lessons to the faithful
as well as faithless all bunkered - home safe,
from all but ordinary inner demons.

Faith
(but is she come?) musters legions of angels,
and I have heard my own Michaelangelo often tonight,
beating back enemies of Him,
the very light of whom they carry.

Today ends the O Antiphons
of Sapientiatide.
O Emmanuel is sung today
in our house and everywhere in Christendom.
Yes, many still believe.

What Do We Have, Really?

We go on
with what we have.

I hear daily about what we do not have,
and I answer with what we have left – consciousness,
culture, knowledge, wisdom, relationships, our very souls –
which is a lot that we have.

Wishing takes us nowhere.
Almost every time I walk into a room of people I am the leader. And,
while I prepare as intelligently as I know how – I am left alone with what I have left.

There is always something new and unexpectedly holy for us all.
Abraham's ram in the bushes
is the always present gift.

Yesterday, I heard men talking at the supermarket – *"Why aren't there more motorized carts here when people need them? Damn all of this!"*

Behind me
the Salvation Army bell rings,
and I move ahead with knowledge
from dreams and experience
that the new,
indeed the Christ is born,
humbly, confident without wishes.

Augean Stables

The hard physical work strengthens me,
or, is it the purification of stripping my studio
back to its bare walls, down to the wooden floor
stretched 85 years ago some 400 sq. feet over Colorado dirt
over what - some crime's lie, the original Blarney Stone,
Al Capone's stash, my sins?

For weeks, maybe a month now obstacles thwarted me,
kept from grasp the great project,
until I felt the aches' honest work:
my prodigal, core muscles rallying my thickish middle:
snatch! and jerk!
with ease this bodacious mass.
Eager, I ponder usefulness; forget what seems clever.

Tomorrow I shall again clean these Augean Stables:
a mess worthy of my failure to await humility
and her angel's invitation.

Upon Waking
During Deep Brain Stimulation Surgery

My fine docs were right…
I am an excellent candidate for this.
I will be under anesthetic
while Dr. Edward West,
my extraordinary neurosurgeon,
drills into my skull.

I awake dreaming –

> Awaking amidst
> interluding forest scenes
> where countless knights
> struggle to turn ancient winches;
> so as to undo complex knots
> that compel forces larger than our
> minds could grasp
> but our tools could unbind.
>
> All this gives way to faces
> staring into my eyes deeply –
> yes, very deeply,
> as if looking into a deep well of mind
> just formed by God, and still forming
> secrets too profound to tell.

My right hand tremor
is already mostly vanished.
It will only get better *"from now on..."*
as Brahms' mighty Requiem flows now
in my memory:
*"Selig sind die Toten die in dem Herren
sterben von nun an...von nun an."*

My head is tightly fastened in a steel
cage held with screws… absolutely rigid.
It really hurts.

I have a ruler written on my face:
1.5mm — 2.00mm — 2.5mm —
marking the target spot:
my Subthalmic Nucleus.

As they sense my awakening,
the Docs ask me for my help.
"Count backwards 10, 9, 8,…"
"what day is today…?"
"who is President…?"
"touch your thumb to your first finger…"

The four hours of surgery
passes as if it were a few minutes.
Dr. West finally asks me
"Is everything OK?"
"Yes," I answer, and fall asleep in a few
seconds.

Awakening in the recovery room,
all Docs seem really energized…
"this will give us lots of options…"
"the procedure went really well…"

I spend the rest of the day and night in
Intensive Care.

Morning now, well before sunrise,
I eagerly "hard wired" await the dawn
and all that confronts me.

*"The night is far spent.
The day draws near
Let us cast off deeds of darkness
And put on the armor of light."*
–Romans 13:12

Sarah, Dr. West's assistant, appears
at the door at 11:00am with the news
"Dr. West said you can go home or spend the night here, it's your call."

Bess and I, riding home,
feel as though a miracle has happened.
Home now,

I sit down and write.

"Eskimo Pies"™

I learned about "Eskimo Pies" at St. Lawrence Church
during my innocent years.
I must have been maybe six or seven years of age when,
on wintry nights, I'd go with my parents
to the church basement Gridiron Club
to buy ice cream from Fr. Schriever.

He'd stand behind a counter of sorts,
sleeves rolled up over hairy arms,
mightily trying to keep up with the rush.
The ice cream pies were about the diameter of a quarter,
and I usually ate one on the way home,
which was across the street.

Years after innocence
I've returned to St. Lawrence Church
many times for concerts and recordings.
Large and elegant, built of Ohio limestone ca.1890,
St. Lawrence looms large over Cincinnati's Price Hill,
still a working-class neighborhood.

I first learned the Latin language there
starting as an altar boy in fourth grade.
At night, I still pray the Rosary
given to me in those days: "to a loyal altar boy."
Sr. Rosetta was our tutor.

In fifth grade, I took some candle wax
(51% pure ritual beeswax) from its overflow place
and stuffed it in one of the many follicles there,
outside in the ancient limestone,
amongst clam shell and fossil.

It remained there for some thirty years undisturbed,
where I'd left it by the altar boys' door.
Gone the last time I checked,
I suppose it has now become,
like Fr. Schriever and Sister Rosetta,
part of the eternal cosmos.

Jungian Dream

Awake, I turn in bed toward the "Dream Catcher" window and fall immediately into a dream.

Carl Jung is right there in front of me.
He shows me what I believe is an old submarine covered in fresh smelling, dark brown canvas.
I assume it is German, stored there from WWII.

As Jung uncovers it, however, it is a thoroughly modern, even futuristic, glass cylinder with much advanced circuitry.

Jung is buoyant and friendly, fit and alert, as he opens the hatch and leads me down into a very deep compartment, going down far below the foundations of our house.

We begin diving very fast, deeper and deeper, going through the eternal depths of the earth, the oceans, the heavens, through time and eons, all at fantastic speed, leaving normal space time.

Finally we stop in the basement. Jung is gone, along with the submarine. I am back where this started, but in the basement.

I wonder if it is time to replace the water heater.

A Bird Spoke to Me Last Night

Last night I dreamt that a bird spoke to me,
reciting a poem he composed in his own tongue.
It was like the Book of Acts, when many people
spoke in different tongues, yet all were understood.

The poem was a melodious one, full of sonorous
sounds and lilting phrases, though I had some difficulty
simultaneously listening and translating
like they do at the United Nations.

Perhaps I was at the United Nations with
the Nation of Birds and there were other birds
also reciting poems, melodious and pleasant sounding.

How I wish I had written down his poem on awakening.
I don't think I can quite remember it - even the concept
is slipping gently away with the morning light.

Stravinsky's *Sacre du Printemps* at 100

Sacre, (like Beethoven's *Grosse Fuge*,
Messiaen's *Quatuor*,
Bach's *Die Kunst*)
will, for me, forever remain
an avant garde piece.

This is permanency, no?
This is permanency in the new:
the life force.
And isn't it so that if rip-offs
by Zappa and other *cognoscendi*
of the new abound,
my point stands?

At peace with them
that war with me,
I wonder at it all,
and secretly
worry too much
about irrelevant things.
That the life force exists
is easily forgotten,
especially by the living.

Raising the dead
has fallen to us, the artists,
ancient and inimitable.
Born into a gold mine,
with heaven at the door,
we miss the Grail Castle
just to the left,
and we've forgotten Parsifal's question
long since.

Sacre's images of pagan Russia
evoke the new
speedily in any hour that we listen,
as bloodily
the century has passed.

Finitude beckons. I'm old.
And good folk called me by name
as one *"steadfast in the faith"*
that Sunday in March
now well passed into memory's deep well.
That permanency
matters at all reveals much
when it ponders loss,
heavy and burdensome:
like death at our door post
without lamb's blood.

Where is our shield and buckler?
We are defeated only if we forget
that loss is not in things,
or people departed;
it is in us. In the deep well
we all contain.

Sacre, it's aboriginal opening,
solo bassoon vine, enwraps us
in tendrils growing
uninformed by ordinary expectation.
Sacre lives on.
Touch it again,
and again it kisses you back.

Those *vigilantes*,
(you know who you are)
who believe that there
should not be a first time for anything,
who don't know that
we are guarding the crib,
must have been fooled this time,
as they always are.

My Room

in St. Charles overlooks a very green, tree'd and fenced
yard. Fallen tree berries color grey shingles
as I look out sitting monastically, score studying
for my 1:45pm church warm-up.

The tall antique iron lamp near my futon,
(a lighthouse in a former life),
was so blinding I opted for a tiny night light
near the gabled, octagon window
to get bearings in the dark.
Another ceramic lamp sits next to me
on a carved wooden stand, hexagon top.

There are old photos of people and horses,
an old embroidered doily (flowers and tatting
I discover, kneeling on the futon.)
Some old lithographs, like those in my grandparents' home,
but these stained, like the doily, are behind me.

James' boyhood letter from Eleanor Roosevelt
sits the prize, over my bed's headboard.

I've sat alone here for about two hours waiting.
Soon I'll be like a horse at the starting gate.
Soon my fingers will race over the white sharps
and black naturals.

Family

This reunion will be different.
You will break the spell,
Which generations in a Maryland glen will tell
Looking through a score,
Twenty years and more
Of unplayed music in a cord of trees.

You had it all along
Along with them which had you.
They knew, but would not tell especially you
Who had them by parts
Too personal.
And your being somehow undid them from within.

Retaliations die.
Love lives which then
And now gives golden weight to your lighter frame.
Deep knowing lets you
Look down from below to see
The God-befriended doves flying free in a chord of trees.

My Heart Dances Her Way – CardioDance 1 & 2

I. January 13, 2015

Dr. Jeffrey Smithfield was my excellent Cardio Doc. *"You have a partial right bundle block, which is typical for a man your age, John. Nothing to worry about, but I should mention it. Have you seen your heart ultrasound? It looks beautiful. Except for the bundle block, I'd say your heart is in perfect shape."*

Indeed, my beating heart did look beautifully graceful, balletic and elegant, sloshing around in fluid, *"ker**Splosh**, ker**Splosh**, ker**Splosh**"* never stopping for these almost 69 years even to go to the toilet.

I thought all was over, but, no… I still must do the Dobutamine Stress Echo Test: *"When, Dr. Smithfield?"*

"Well. John, we can't take you until February 10. I want to do the test, because Dr. West asked that I sign off on this."

Yes, another delay.

Mara, the appointment gal, promised to call if there's a cancellation.

I say *"W(hat)hiskey, T(he)ango, F(uck)oxtrot?"* and I imagine I'll say it again.

"W(hat)hiskey, T(he)ango, F(uck)oxtrot?"

Dr. Smithfield looked at me squarely. *"You really ought to get a stationary bicycle and start exercising."*

I'll do it. I like him. And I know just where I'll put it in the studio.

It feels now like it'll be Fourth of July before all this is done.

II. One week later

An Elephant on my chest, an elephant never met, in hiding awaits me. Undress'd to the waist on Monica's orders, I wait, as a soldier for battle.

How did all these kids get here? I wonder, inquiring about her age: *"well, let's say less than thirty"* all Copenhagen blonde, and all business, Monica is a thistle in a lab coat.

"I'm here to watch your blood pressure – 132/80, perfect. Do you smoke?"

The very heavens will descend on him.

Bonnie, my ultrasound gal, is an undiscarded Christmas tree in her red flannel, snowman print pullover shirt. She was sweating like a cotton picker in August.

Helga would administer my intravenous drugs. She speaks excellent English with a tart Finnish accent, knows about Sibelius, even recognized the 2nd and 4th Symphony themes, Finlandia, but botches three IV attempts in my wrist before sinking one into my arm where they draw blood.

Dr. Gregory Smithfield arrives like an Eagle Scout off to war as he pulls back the tent-like curtain/door, clearly in command:

"OK, let's go, start with 20mg. John, we'll take your heart beat all the way to 132 bp, then we'll be done."

On the way to 110, watching my beautiful heart on the ultrasound screen, I see the Holy Grail, I float off to Solyma, home.

"Yes, Blissful life suffuses ev'ry limb
And when one opens up an ancient, parchment scroll,"

I feel a painful throat lump, like some reflux; it's worse at 112, 113…
chest pain at 115, 116, 117…
120 (pain), 122 (more pain and fear, too)
125 (an elephant is in the room), 130 (she sits on my chest, and stays, and stays) 130, 128, 126 …

"How much longer, Dr. Smithfield?"
and it is past.

"You did great, John. We're done."
Dr. Smithfield huddles with Helga, reads through a fist-full of EKG stuff, all mine.

"I'd like to take your case to my weekly meeting with my colleagues. Then, I'll sign off with approval for your DBS."

Sunny afternoon's January greets me as the Grail Castle fades from apprehension. I remain a knight of the realm, a boyish 68, my initiation centuries past. I'd just minutes ago again looked into my fears' eyes, he blinked, vanished in the light.

The Chronicle of Change

If I tried to chronicle change, I'd be likely to stumble onto something (chew on it like a prized acorn blustered onto by a squirrel in winter, all shaking his booty for us to see).

He discovers another Blarney Stone for the common man, and somewhere there must be encoded what *cognoscendi* tell us must exist:

"The one, truly authentic, extraterrestrial Blarney Stone," I call it.

Or, better still
"Four or five easily understood paths to enlightenment."

Let's try again with a true story.

My friend Jack Sanford and I went hiking in the Mojave Desert in search of an ancient fresh water spring, long since thought lost in antiquity.

Without a map or compass we hiked silently for about half a day.

Jack led us to a tiny trickle of water, hidden in plain sight to all except those with eyes to see.

Now, Jack exfoliated, the story that indeed this tiny trickle of water was enough to support a family of people – provided it could be found – was compelling.

And, that the missionaries dug wells which eventually dried causing these people to forget the ancient "trickle" and eventually die was indeed compelling.

Jack and I hiked home as the sun set. And my greatest life mentor, saying few words, taught me the profound lesson of how to stay alive amongst the Blarney Stones and to survive the impulse to revert to obviousness.

On that day I learned
the chronicle of change.

Thoughts Rambling on Monday Night

In the studio I sit in shorts and sneakers. I wonder what keeps the work
so far from me.
There is a wall somehow between us. Those tasks I've set myself
call to me and I don't listen, don't answer. It cumulates like gray clouding
always "over there" about four feet away. I must step into the mass of it somehow. Maybe tonight will find me courageous. At least I've outlined that my work consists just now in six projects:

> opera, organ practice, conducting, organ recording, poems, reading. Can I do a little each day? Sobered as I think about all this

I get anxious and sometimes shake in bed falling asleep. Wanting to be worthy I work and am content with the little rewards of some good double thirds, a bar of good scoring, my map of takes for the final recording edit, a journal entry like this one.

Talking to my painful restlessness now for about an hour I'm calm. It seems that I've spent the better part of today digging myself out. June 12, 2000.

The Boychoir music director auditions were today. I've gone down a path since those days that's led to more and more solitary work.

It's cool in the studio tonight, and very quiet. I'll sort some scores gone astray, read some Latin in a while and probably stay away from the phone. I don't dare let my energy direct herself too much away from the work.

Mehmet Ali Agca was pardoned today for shooting the Pope, and I wonder what the Holy Father is thinking just now.

Transition to Final Things

In the workshop today I spot a small piece of wood on the floor.

To know its identity.
I needn't pick it up, look closely,
no.

I've known this 3/4" squarish piece some 50 years now, when one day it broke off from the pig-shaped cutting board (the pig's "hind" foot) some 20 years ago. I remember repairing it then, but how often or when the last time evades memory.

Seeing that little pig's foot on the floor, I panic for a second, think *"I've lost the board,"* this precious heirloomed common woodpiece, worn by my many deep cuts through onions, carrots, chickens, hog schmizzl.

I spin around and the pig is there where I'd placed it who knows, 10 years ago?

Looking, I can remember my fingers' touch on those small valleys in the wood (where a live pig's bacon would be), scrubbed with SOS™ pads umpteen times in soapy water while someone and someone else talked about the ordinary things that a household hears.

 It's 4th of July weekend in a few days, and out of respect I'll fix the little pig's leg again, not one more time, but one time more, and maybe he deserves a place on the wall now, deserves to move from utility to love.

Surfaces

Surfaces inhabit my attention and beckon for respect.
I treat surfaces as storage areas,
and I fill with regret when I load them down.
Does everyone have piles surrounding them?
Just looking now at my desk I see:

1. 12 books
2. wallet
3. meds (6 containers)
4. magnifying glass
5. water glass
6. blood pressure cuff
7. clock/radio
8. Rolodex™
9. bookend
10. eye-glasses
11. eye-glass cleaner
12. car keys
13. file folder storage gizmo
14. computer (50 items on desktop)
15. 2-octave keyboard
16. dirty handkerchief
17. pocket knife
18. scissors
19. pen
20. pencil
21. to-do list
22. hand-copied Latin phrases
23. mouse pad
24. mouse
25. three-hole paper punch
26. Jackson Jeffries business card
27. a small lamp
28. numerous electrical wires
29. a small electric fan
30. a book mark
31. three receipts
32. a magazine promotional piece
33. a flashlight
34. 2 coasters, one with glass atop

I say again: Egad,
Buckminster Fuller saw surfaces where others saw objects,
like Euclid who failed to grasp the full import of his
geometric "games" as Bucky lampooned.

I hear objects; and they always float on surfaces. That is
how I hear my compositions before writing.

"I was just at the Grail Castle door, and then it was gone, as if it just slipped away." – Parsifal, on his Grail quest.

"I t'ought, I t'aw a puddy tat! I did, I did! I t'aw a puddy tat!"
– Tweety the bird, speaking of Sylvester, the cat.

There is something here, an epistemology of forms
perhaps, that I need to understand; something deep
beneath the surface.

Claude's Software of the Soul

Claude's coat, all black and snow white, reminds me of a Holstein cow's patterning: unmistakable but difficult to recall, and seeming to shapeshift.

As these events began fifteen months ago, he was small enough to curl into a large coffee mug. And now, he's a heavyweight, lovable, 13-pound lug with a ton of heart still wrap't in Holstein snow ocean with jet black continents.

As a kitten Claude frolicked and wrestled with abandon together with his sibling, Camille. They joined our family in November, 2013. The emotional time clock was re-set.

And apart from this fun, alone at 15 years of age, our senior cat, Basil, was well into patrician, Maine Coon loftiness. Basil slept in his furnace room bed, still connected to us, but doing little. The long since tenured Basil was not amused by the new energy. And he failed all efforts at feigned invisibility.

On the other hand, Claude sought Basil with gestures of love, such that his intentions penetrated Basil's force field poco a poco.

Claude would lay himself tummy up, within whispering distance of a clearly annoyed great one. Claude, setting himself, again tummy up, would strategically position himself in a hallway such that he seem'd to be saying "this is Claude's Corner, please pay the toll, or I'll kiss you."

A year has passed.

Basil has been transformed from lonely curmudgeon into a new spirit that allows and supports his duly earned, age appropriate dignity.

Neither cat has lost anything.

So, my question is: how did young Claude know all this?

He seem'd pre-packaged with, well, healing wisdom.

Aren't we all created hard wired for love?

Pygmies

Pygmies blow darts poison at me.
they hide in tall grass
without the stature or the courage to say

I am:

Darts prick here
They there know them too
I stand my ground wait,
me, like a rattlesnake.

Madly turning it over and over
Like some damned moral theologian
As if to think the truth more deadly
than the dart.

To know one's accusers: isn't that a right?
Writ down somewhere on skin or parchment old?

I'm told that criminals in courts
don't have to face this sport
but hypocrisy and humor weirdly marry
in my daily living
I tarry and wonder why
the arrow didn't hit me as thoughts flew by.

What Isn't Obvious at the Buffalo Grill

My Uncle Bill (the one my Dad
used to beat up in the coal bin),
my Uncle Bill would have loved
The Buffalo Grill.

At the corner of Colfax and Spruce,
The Buffalo Grill stands in proud,
shabby greasiness
much as it has some
50 Memorial Days ago,
the years passing her by,
she remains unchanging.

My Uncle Bill
would really irritate my dad:
*"See John, what I want is my own
greasy spoon, y'know, good food,
good people."* But this isn't the why
of the coal bin sessions.

Bess and I enter
and walk past a young man being
served the $4.50 breakfast burrito
smothered in sausage gravy.

It was the size of a rolled up
Sunday newspaper.
What wonders held promise inside?
I order the American omelet
with all the trimmings.
Bess went with her more civilized
French Toast.

The regulars at the counter
and at tables looked like a hired cast,
but their knowing stares at us were
as real and powerful,
clean as a rifle barrel,
and potent as four fingers
of Wild Turkey 101.

I imagined these regulars
were released from asylums
for holiday breakfast, no:
Seminarians of the true
church. Wrong again.

They were angels, sent to cure me of
obviousness, my ever present enemy.

Candie,
sunken chest and eyeballs,
wore overpowering
eau d'ordinaire
such that my sinuses
were cleared, and my ship sails filled
as we walked into the morning sun.
But there is more.

My Uncle Bill wanted one thing more
besides "Bill's Greasy Spoon."
He'd tell me
*"Jack, I'd like to go to Spain,
get a burro, and travel around Spain."*
Now this, too, really incensed JK senior,
and did it so much more
than the drunken binges that
led to the coal bin.

Well, now
my Uncle Bill really did this,
as we learned when a telegram arrived
saying Uncle Bill Kuzma
had died in Spain
buried
in an unmarked spot.
And in my mind's eye
I have often and long visited
this soul mate's grave;

an obvious wish,
no? And I'd sing
"In Paradisum."

At Colfax and Spruce
life continues at the Buffalo Grill.
A waitress arranges her blouse
so that whoever wanted
could meander past the
cheap G clef neck tattoo on to
her obvious mysteries.

Prostate Trouble

With my PSA at 6.5, my internist thinks I should have the prostate ultrasound and biopsy. The urologist, Dr. Terrance, is maybe early 40's : *"drop down and bend over. OK here's some tissue to clean off, I'll be in my office."* He continues, *"one in three have cancer with your profile. We can wait six months and do this again, or do the biopsy now. My call, I'd do it. Bring someone to take you home, I don't want you driving home looking down at your dick."* Three weeks after that was last Tuesday, Tuesday of Holy Week. The slim, butch, olive skinned nurse asks me - *"Did you do your enema and take the first antibiotic pill?"*

Yes.

"And no aspirin the last week?" No, none.

"Feel constipated?"

I never really thought about it. *"Well, most men don't."* Lying on my left side, Dr. Terrance inserts the probe. This thing goes into your rectum and from there the ultrasound views your prostate. The biopsy comes later, but now they talk about my prostate. *"You've got a few stones in there. No big deal. I see no obvious signs of cancer."* Then the biopsy.

Nurse inserts the 15" needle into the probe: *"don't worry, we don't stick it all the way in."* Gee. I'm zapped with rapid needle insertions into my prostate, through my colon. There will be 10.

First time is OK, like an inner tube thwack on the bottom that goes through to your testicles. By the 5th I'm ready to stop, it's like Dr. Fu Man Chu's torture chamber now. Finally, I stumble off the table, covered in sweat, table too.

"Clean up and I'll come back for you," says Dr. Terrance. I go home sobered and very sure of my mortality. Thursday the news comes: no cancer.

By Saturday afternoon I'm feeling groin pain.

I'm sure, and turns out I'm right - it's a urinary infection, like Santa Barbara in 1976. In the emergency room, Dr. Willis Petersen is about 40 I'd say, and I expect that he's working Easter Eve for some reason - extra money, or maybe he's low on the food chain. He's really getting a perverse thrill treating a prostate biopsy recovery. *"Any penile discharges?"*

My pants down, I'm covered "down there" with a gown. He probes, rubber gloved, into my soreness. I feel like an elephant's sitting on my genitalia. One more rectal/prostate feel and I'm done. *"Can you pee for us?"* Sure.

Man, it's a lot cloudier than I realized, looking at it in the plastic cup.

"Just blood, no pus." Egad.

I wait an hour and read about Ramakrishna, wondering if he or other great hermits ever went through this. *"Well, your urine specimen was very interesting."* Really?

"You have a lot going on down there."

I took the pills right away, and it was morning before the pain left, Easter morning.

I conduct like the boyish 54 that I am. I think I'll have a drink this afternoon.

Dream Song for Uncle Bill Kuzma

Jack hears music, mostly his own,
and others' mainly.
But when silence plays music,
it is the loudest Jack ever hears.

Uncle Bill knew Jack, liked him and hated music loud.
"The ignorant, the stupid,
when they crank their music, they crank it real loud."

Now Uncle Bill was a sort of poet type,
and he got a burro and wandered through Spain mostly.
He also got drunk and then got dead.
They told young Jack it was from the "D.T's",
Jack shivered when he heard:
Uncle Bill dead, and what "D.T's" meant.

And Jack hated the crassness
they put on Uncle Bill's whole life.
Low, they, compared to him.
Dad paid for his gravestone somewhere in Spain.
Jack wondered about the burro, and an uncle who loved him,
and the loudest silence the world now hears.

Ancient Warriors' Song

A log watched ants rage
red 'gainst black on grey weather'd wood
in a dappled mountain forest.

They would kill on
'til the dusk I watch'd
as hours and hours fell
a day not yet summer.

Ancient questions and trees
speak 'gainst quiet colors,
aground, whom twigs hear
warriors alive or no?

Pain, terrible pain
I imagine black on red wrings those jaws
terrible and ancient.

Ignominiously carried down
into rotting wood the fallen go.
Were they brave, and does life beyond
still this hill command them?

Yes, and today's voices tell that they were here
struggling before my own cold bed
found the woods' words today
silent and deadly.

Unbearable Nostalgia

Unbearable nostalgia
grips me ghosts in audience surround
where music was before echoes now abound

An ancient campsite once
now spoke me the same tune
my mother dead I'm in my father's room

A basement nook shelves
full of obsolete condensers, wires,
currents carried replace the big seegars.
An electrical man, I adopted this home
where once a common man, woman, son tried,
got something going.

The empty church on Easter afternoon,
the stadium crowds gone
cheers, alleluias boom louder when I alone
ages hence, walking, whose
memories of resting test
a faith that knows music's life was here.

Jack Mad with Music

Dreamed 'bout Jack tonight,
Jack mad with music, the artist young.
Time was always Jack played music
Electronic organs mostly at first
Easy he thought to hide that way and he learned it young.

There was a visiting choir and ours
Singing double chorus motets and such
But because Jack had hidden so much
he would only watch and touch
keys others knew not, as such
But tried, missed, for hours.

Girls mostly, priest-bound guys
sang with us, but missed many beats,
Their teachers made excuses
but Jack hated them
quoting in hallowed rules their hollowness.
Jack knew, but kept quiet.

Afraid at Night

One night dreams don't come
Jack knows spirits wise live
somewhere to inspire or to console.
No one speaks tonight
all is still in spite
of incantations humble to my soul

Can inner muse and music
ever stop loud silence
bathing triple forte in Jack's ear?
Can my will rescue him
from ancient spirit's voice?
Bed rock, shiver, pulse, no, my dear.

Things go bump in the night
Let Jack have his dream,
as he asked in childhood it would seem

So now a man
rounded by no sleep
he is such stuff as dreams are made on.

Committee Meeting

Jack was stupified
while trivialities dogmatized
filled the church's basement air to thicken'd

opining skulls' ears wide
Point of order! Point of ……
Where is Joe McCarthy when we need him?

Everywhere it seem'd to me.
Jack was quiet, still, unborn,
while swine devoured, swilled, his silent pearls,
he hides baskets of them under,
A light shines, sure, ok.
But who will ever know him?
Or again be like he?

Rapt and by their very tails
Jack held them speechless, speaking
finally, and forever in their memories, home,
now they hear him, and they think
"Jack move, and how?"
And sometimes he moves on when all else fails.

The Thing Itself I'll Be

The thing itself I'll be
star, rock, tree
I'll find no better models than these three

Cynical stander-by
selfish pretender, I.
Weep, weep away the stain, Jack, cry.

The sound should be filled with tears
without crying, Music
flowing tears sheds life and someone dying

Ego, witless fool
die, else lovers never
tears to shed, and loving die together

But what am I except
a passer-by who kept
a watch to see Jack's magic lantern lit?

The thing itself he'll be
has been from eternity
That heav'n and earth in little space shall be.

Faust's Seeker

Dawn and toil your covenant
on earth of me requiring,
with gin and scotch me firing.
Coro grande, coro piccolo
fierce and tender passion
wrings with effort still unspent.

The search for Faust call it up
Who, and in whom Lucifer shall speak
of mysteries delectable, sweet
but wise. And to the great high GOD
shall his thoughts crow and cow.

In lines six each of notes and words
shall this son's search be found
for all Odyssians to come sing rounds
of ecstasy. O rota aeterna turn,
for sweating me who sees only shades.
Light ever flickers from blades.

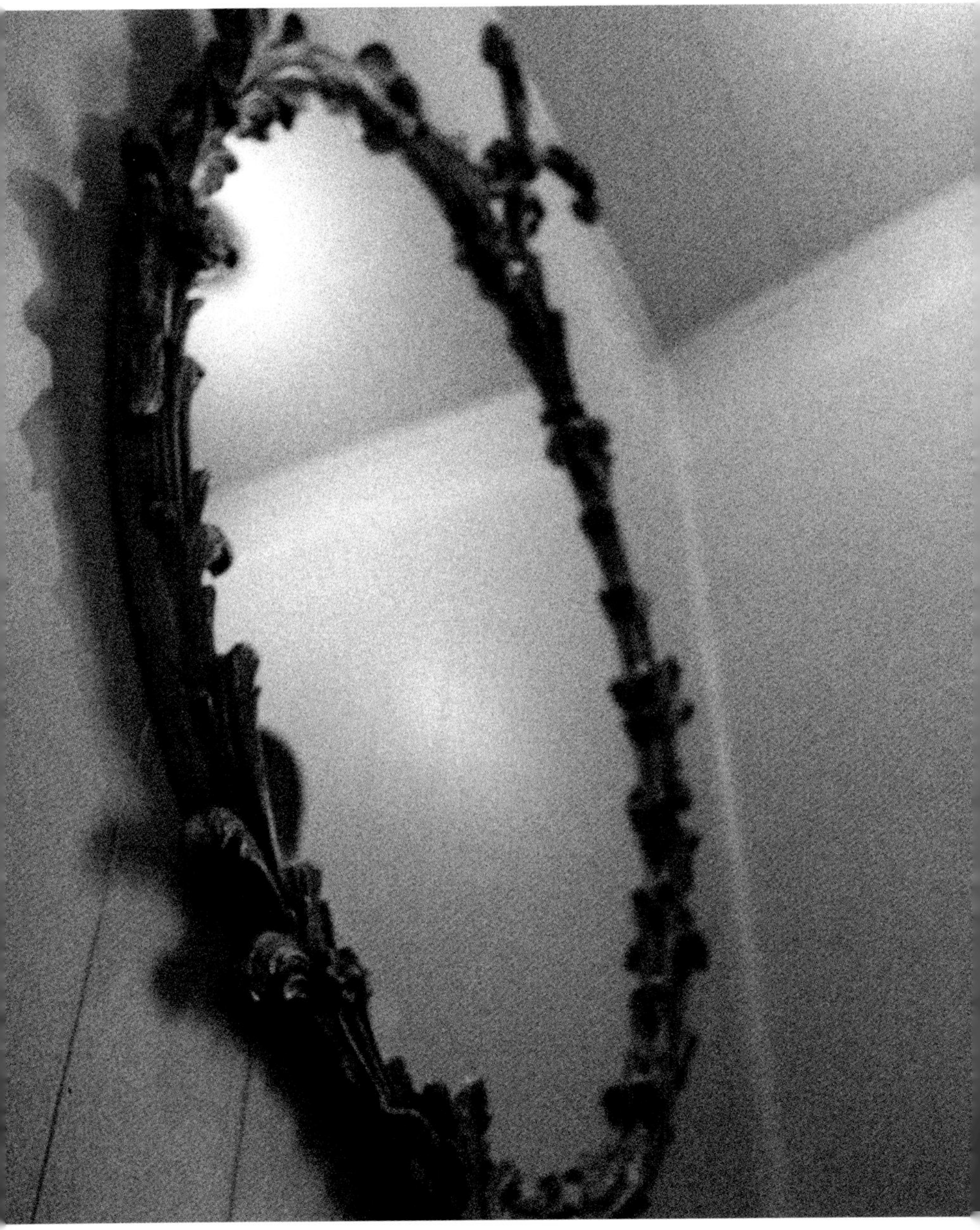

The Mirror...

…had been packed at the funeral home.
my childhood heirloom mirror
would accompany us
to our new Denver home,
some thirty years ago now.

This elegant mirror had hung
in our apartment since I was a boy.

Gaudy, in that Victorian way…
always high fashion,
all overstated magnificence,
she parries her would-be detractors with her
secret weapon of beautiful reflection amplified
by gold framing of the subject in question.
"Who is the fairest of them all?"
becomes her question, too.

She holds a prominent position —
some would say "holds court" now,
above the landing leading to my studio
where, sunlit, one can take
her unique tour of those privileged souls,
eager to see into her vast mysteries.

She always evokes laughter:
outrageous in all her affirmation of our pride.

This is why we love her so,
and why holidays and gatherings
made more festive by mirrors,
give us what we all seek:
a true reading of the face we present to the world.

Yes, a face reflected in honesty,
always free of flattery,
and full of truth.

Ubiquitous Genius

Painting pros jostle
at the hardware store paint counter
early Friday morning.

Master of all he surveys, his name tag
BILL, "ASK ME, 'CAUSE I'M THE BOSS"
explains his dismissal of class struggle,
and addresses me with respect due
a fellow soldier in battle:
"high heat car paint? We don't carry it.
If you just want to paint a grill,
or fireplace, we've got a deal on that.
Hell, this Som'bitch'll take you up to 1200 degrees!"

I accept his solution,
walk to check out,
nod my thanks.
Bill knowingly winks back –
"no problem, comrade."

Pate of Foie Gras

Francois wore a medal on a ribbon around his neck.
I've forgotten now what honor this indicated,
but he wore it with pride,
and Francois was proud of Casablanca,
where he greeted us every week or so.
There was another restaurant, just opened,
and we asked about it.

"Well, I ordered the foie gras,
and after a long time, he asked me
'how was the foie gras,'
and I said to heem 'I am steel weeting for eet'
and he said 'but you have fineeshed eet,'
 and I said to heem
'the menu says foie gras, wheech I like very much,
what you have served me is pate of foie gras.'
So I would not recommend thees place at all."

Francois' standards were high.
He had a falling out, finally,
with Marin's husband, the owner,
and he was gone at our next visit.
Everything at Casablanca changed
and the once mighty Lobster fra Diavolo
became a real mess covered in a chicken liver sauce.
Next we knew, Casablanca closed,
and reopened some weeks later,
Francois commanding the day.
He invited us to the reopening where
a whole calf was being carved in the main room
and where his cousin played classical piano music
with great skill and elegance to match the food
and triumph of the night.
We slowly drifted apart,
moved to Princeton finally, and I expect
we'll meet again somewhere,
his medal in place, and we'll talk of the old times.

Scents

It was the scent of my old score
that impressed the task's nature on me.
I remember it from Cincinnati long ago.
I'd wander and browse at Acres of Books
on cloudy Cincinnati Saturdays.
Once looking at an old book there I
read: *"the artist's work
is in the nature of making,
and not of knowing. Knowing
is properly the work of Philosophy."*

Well now.

And that scent of old books
now lived in my Bach Trio Sonatas,
as I play number six in G major for the
first time in thirty years.
How I used to breeze through
these sublime measures!
And would I pass an Eastman senior
organ jury today, I wonder?

Having come far in my rehabilitation
I now can play a program with some
confidence, I've recorded some good
things, and I know that the re-step of
those traces has worked, and I know I
need to go to a simpler layer that the
old pages sniffed out for me. Just how
do I play the organ?

And reading Dupre's humblingly
original 79 Chorales, I feel my hips and
hands adjusting to old synapses' firings?
I'd swear to it. And I wonder along
the way about Dupre's "grand legato"
and his tablaturistic fingerings and
pedalings.

Yes, this is, was, my path, through these
romantic French organists, through
Parvin Titus, through Gordon Franklin,
through Craighead, and Viderø to me.

And I know now that there was a
wisdom beyond my headstrong anger
that drove me against all that trendiness
and away from academic security.

I remember long Saturdays learning
these simple things, and I'm trusting
that some pathway back lies in me and
that in my small life left to me I can
know something permanent about this
artifact of me that started with the attic
accordion at St. Lawrence corner.

Come to think of it, that book that I used
to teach myself had a smell too. That
book long ago disappeared but smells
and their memories remain.

How like me all this is, and how I hope
it leads me again to larger things, and
how this was ever placed here in this life
for me to find is my treasured mystery.

Auntie

Auntie and I are out at lunch together.
"I'm out at lunch with Auntie,
my aging caretaker,"
I tell the waiter.

"Auntie takes me
out for lunch on the days
I am released from
the Asylum."

Our waiter, Miles today,
was ready for his usual greeting:
"Hi, I'm Miles,
and I'll be your waiter today,"
when Auntie and I begin our show.

For some 26 years, we've performed
this act, Auntie and I:
"Why, I used to drink out of the
bottle, until Auntie rescued me."
I'd deliver my improvised lines
just loud enough to draw attention
from other diners.

And, we all know how Auntie hates
having the spotlight on her!

Auntie is peripatetic, a peregrine,
a wanderer around this place,
Sunday mornings especially.
She loves to wander into the choir room:
"Officer on the Bridge!" I'll say,
and there she is, all performer,
chiming in,
and blessing us with a prayer
and more.

I'll miss all this,
and more.

I'll miss the parts of
Being that Auntie carries.

She carries these so authentically,
so deeply as to
live these things out
for the rest of us.

Isn't it so,
that some individuals
are so alive,
so connected with authenticity,
that they
are "originals" inimitable,
and unmatched?

Auntie, we will feel
inconsolable in our loss
of these days with you,
because you have penetrated
so deeply into our souls
and into our hearts
that you have become
part of our spirits,
part of our psychology.

When we miss you and say so,
we will be
telling the truth of loss.

But there is more.
What we'll be missing is most deeply
and authentically missing
in us.

And the empty spaces can be filled
only with the passing of time.
Yes, we will move on;
but never the same again.

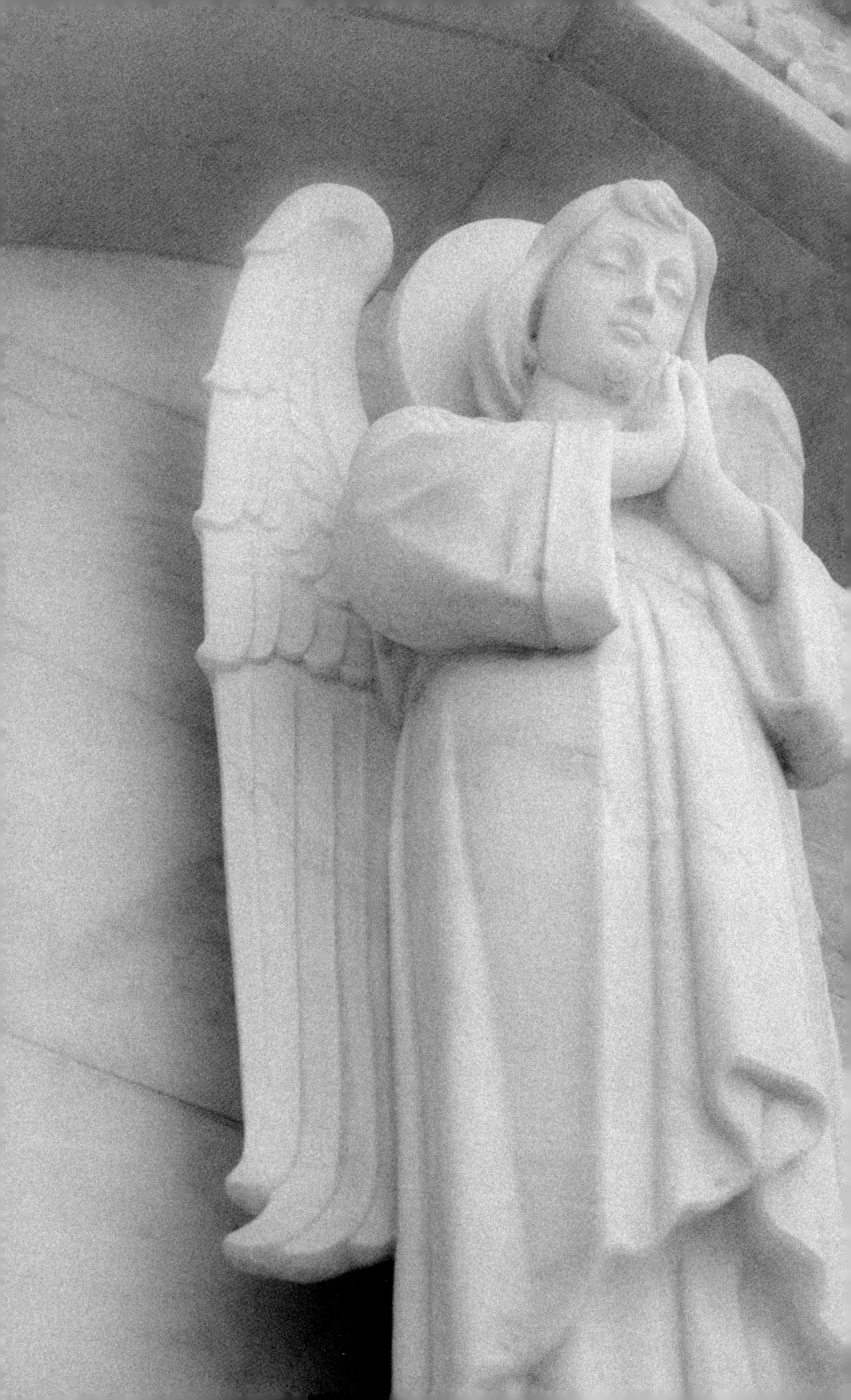

Jack's Catenary Curve

Jack ponders
his retirement announcement.
A boyish 68 years old,
up early at 2:09am
he's working to finish the finale of his new Requiem:
Tarantella Ecstasse.

Jack is astonished.

As if told by an angel,
Jack knows that re: subjects and objects
- all knowledge finds us before we find knowledge
- there is never enough waiting,
  only too much
- life is mostly ahead, important
  past life only clarifies (gee,
  will he live to be 136, when all crows shed plumage?)

Jack knows too, that there is no time for
- any thematic catalog
- retro of any kind
- encomia ipsium

Having promised much to others,
Jack owes little for all the recklessness.
Sweat equity, paid in advance
from his own thesaurus meritorium
earned by humbling
and many years' work
(and Jack needs humbling),
some gold is in the bank.

Sweating like a slave cotton picker,
Jack earns his soul
feeling the tumbler notches
fall into place,
a slash here and there,
concatenation has been happening.

Intellectual property indeed.

Ιεροσόλυμα

In the dream I am lecturing
to a small group that I don't know.
At the blackboard I write
Ιεροσόλυμα. Jerusalem.

I'd learned this word at age 17,
in Fr. Hussey's Greek class one morning,
probably in 1963, at Elder High School.
I can hear him say it in my memory: Ιεροσόλυμα

During the Judas Maccabaeus rehearsals,
the lyric sung by Donald and Susan
in the Tenor/Soprano duet:
"O Solyma, O Solyma." haunted me.
And Handel's aching anapest setting in c minor
drove the words deeply into me. Solyma.

Now, that sounded so, so familiar.
I looked in my Webster unabridged,
the one with onionskin pages.
No. I looked in my Webster Collegiate,
the one Aunt Cathyrne gave me for First Communion.
No again. I looked in the pronouncing gazeteer,
the listing of biographical and geographical names, no.

It was a few nights later after our Judas performance
had sounded her last notes that the dream came to me,
"unbidden, rising up through the common."

And I wrote Ιεροσόλυμα on the blackboard.
The Holy City, where the Pope,
frail and swaying, prayed at the wall a few days before.
The Nova Solyma has been a part of me from the start.

The Fly

The Fly had been floating in my water glass
when I saw her motionless awaiting rescue, alive
as I saw her grasp my tissue's dry island's rescue.

She stayed only ten seconds or so,
furiously drying her wings.
Then, airborne again, she flew
out the open door, away from me –
never again to be seen by me,
unreflective about this wonderment that surrounds us
here and now as space/time's eternal mystery puzzles me.

Solitude and Friendship

Solitude has been a refuge
since childhood.
I have always felt safest when alone,
and solitude itself was a childhood
secret known only to me.

Parents quickly sensed this
and were angered by my secret.
While perfectly innocent,
they hunted me down
if they thought I was hiding.
I didn't feel guilty, nor was I
objectively guilty of wrong doing.
Nonconformity and secrecy
were my crimes.

I lived in a Cincinnati funeral home
from early infancy until college.
The large 1911 house had four levels:
    Basement - laundry, workshop,
        coal bin, etc.,
    Main floor - visitation rooms
    Upper floor - apartments
    Attic - storage

I never felt "safely alone" unless
I had an empty floor between
me and any others. Nevertheless,
hiding places were plentiful as
Bluegills in any Ohio pond.

Since most people do not crave solitude,
their hiding places are often in full view,
hidden from eyes that do not see.
Anyone who has lived with a cat
will attest to this*.

Children are expert artists at this as well.
I'd add nesting birds, bats, bees,
spiders, and any animal near death.

An organist by vocation,
the solitude of practice alone in the
sacred space was ecstatic and healing.
To this day it remains a legitimate
reason for solitude if Pharisees
were to comment.

Solitude in childhood
led to meditation which remains
my most important teacher.
Out of the void comes wisdom not
sought and not verbal.
I am blissfully aware of all things,
and I know the awful grace of God.

I nevertheless treasure time with my wife
(even if we are both absorbed
in solitary things),
time with friends, colleagues, etc.,
time away from and in all this solitude.

Friendship is the only thing that we
choose, and friendship, like marriage,
remains the vehicle through which
I experience the most intense,
transformative, passionate wholeness
and primal energy.

Solitude, however, is never chosen,
but chooses us. And as I age,
solitude seeks me out,
with a holy beckoning of truths too
precise for words. Only plain awareness
and resonance of the eternal remains.

*A friend once told me "wherever you walk outdoors, a cat is watching."

Organ Music at Cincinnati's "Old Odeon"

The "Old Odeon" auditorium
was the site of organ recitals
during my high school years.

Somewhere in Cincinnati's
western downtown,
I don't remember exactly where,
I went usually on Sunday afternoons
to hear Wayne Fischer's students
"bravely play at the Old Odeon"
as a critic once said.

I heard John Weisrock
play Bach's 5th Trio Sonata,
and the Reger BACH, I think.
I know I heard him play
Franck's Piece Heroique, too,
maybe on another program.
Ritter Werner played
there, I believe, and Bill Catherwood.

The organ sat buried
behind facade pipes,
and I think it was a Hillgreen-Lane.
The sound was right in your face
in a thick curtained, dead theater.
It was the first time I recall
hearing any real reed tone,
and all of the students played
from memory.

No Parvin Titus "pupils"
(as he called them)
ever played there during my years.
They played in the auditorium
at the Shillito mansion
at Highland and Oak Streets.

There was a divide between the studios
like, I suppose, the divide of later years.

The Fischer students all seemed very
tightly wound, like Wayne.
The Titus students seemed a bit aloof.

Wayne's students
were unapologetic virtuosos.
Both teachers had excellent players.

Wayne was a pockmarked
emaciated man
looking a bit cadaverous while
Parvin Titus was all propriety:
patrician in his speech and bearing.

I loved the programs
and the secular setting. I went alone,
sat alone, knew no one, and always left
immediately after the concert's end.

It was wonderful.

I'd emerge never disappointed,
having heard great organ playing,
with some of Sunday afternoon left.

And I can still hear those tightly
tuned reeds in an unforgiving space.

What ever happened to that organ,
and those days?

Hard

I just closed my music file
stopping the opera scoring for a bit
to record some words so much slower than the

hard
driving me
onward
toward what

hard for me
to leave home on concert tour

hard
the reckoning of my small contribution to art

hard
these inner note groups that confront me

hard
the alcohol on my soft tissues

hard
these plastic keys against soft fingers

hard
heartbeat in my ear-drums' shake

hard
this Bildungsroman snapshot that haunts me

hard
the rocky place that gets more narrow with each dream

how hard am I?

Composers' Panel

"He came out of nowhere,"
I heard someone whisper
as I was introduced on the Composers' Panel.

I should have known better
than to join anything, especially something called a "panel."

And I imagine now that whispers like this have followed
me many places. I expect this as I get older and know more,
but early on, I just fought them off,
threw them off when they tried to pile on.

It's too late for them now, too late to teach me the wrong
ways. I've been through too much enemy fire, too many
darts blown at me by pygmies hiding in the tall grass.

It's too late for the wounds to matter now, not because of
unusual toughness so much as inner magic with her large
shields of painful memory.

In a dark place for so long one finds the light easily, and we
never return to Plato's cave however often we're dragged
down to the entrance where false gods reward others.

And it makes me wonder about accolades, remembering
that Vaughan-Williams even turned down knighthood
along with all honorary degrees.

He came late to it all, as I have, and the lateness of others'
attentions matters little at a late age, whenever we reach it.

I heard that the Buddha was born fully aged from his
mother's womb.

I continue as a maker of small things working on through
the dark and reflecting what light has followed me from the
start, before it was too late.

From Cosmo
Astrologer to Melchior, Balthazar, and Caspar

I watch the stars tonight as I have for decades now.
Learning for my master's advantage
as they take from this and that which I observe:
that the heavens and we live one life,
drawn from the deep well of ancient experience,
beyond wonder, and eloquently retold night after night.

I call them by name, these "constellations",
telling of battles that raged before time.

I am Cosmo,
astrologer to Melchior,
Balthazar,
and Caspar.

On a special journey, I say,
(and they argue with me) but they follow the star,
as only I and fellow sky watchers know how.

The camels and I are aging.
and with them, I know a bit of eternity.

Something on the ground,
earthly,
but bright as heaven, is shining brightly now.

It is just ahead,
and we must bear the darkness only a little longer.

A Monk of the Abbey

The autumn mornings
of 1961 seemed
filled with promise.
Out of bed by 5:00,
a cup of instant coffee
(always with hot tap water)
downed at the kitchen sink,
and I was out the door,
walking a mile or so
to St. William's church.

Six o'clock Mass beckoned,
and by 5:45 I'd read the
Ordo Missae,
had chatted with Fr. Hussey,
and was in place at the organ
ready to chant the ancient
mystifications again,
as I'd done since age nine.

I'd known all the Vatican Kyriale chants
since fifth grade, and I remember
my favorites to this day,
fifty-three years later:

Missa Cum Jubilo,
    Orbis factor,
    Cunctipotens,
    Pro defunctis,
    De angelis.

And then there were
    Dies Irae,
    Lauda Sion Salvatorem,
    Stabat Mater,
    Victimae paschali laudes,
    Veni Creator Spiritus,
    Pange lingua gloriosi,
    Salve Regina,
    In Paradisum,
    Pueri Hebraeorum,
    Adoro Te Devote …

Egad:
*"What would my life have been,
without their faithful and
harmonious company?"**

My ordination on Easter Eve, 1958,
when I was lifted up by the great
light followed a postulancy
and novitiate of my own making.
I have been a Monk of the Abbey
since those days,
and I have known without doubt
my life's course with God
that began unbidden during
those innocent years of
singing Gregorian chants
at some 8,000 masses.

I just said Matins and Lauds,
and as my days lengthen
into eternity,
I'll always know
the music of heaven.

* Gian Carlo Menotti: "The Unicorn, the Gorgon, and the Manticore"

Rolodex™

Late tonight
and out of musical ideas for now
I flip through my Rolodex™
looking for something I miss
here and now.
Many shysters and others emerge
in my reflections on these names,
and I wonder
how this was collected over many years.

false gods
living short lives
in my vanity here recorded.
Things once deemed important
loom large here in my own smallness
scribbled into these cards in hope
that something big would happen
sometime.

I take a mighty slug of Scotch
and know that some culling is in order.
And life subsides for me preferring
health for this moment's reflection as
the end of my life and times is before
me here, in my Rolodex.™

Earlier today, I went through
an old travel brochure from
the Copenhagen days,
now 33 years ago.

All this still means something to me,
and my address book is much older
than I, who lives another day.

Ecclesiad

A greasy spoon near my house
smells of frying bacon notably
in the early morning.

This comforts me.

There seem'd to be more smells when I was a boy.
More caterpillars,
more leaves.

And a good stick is almost impossible to find now.

Those childhood mornings at St. Lawrence corner
smelled like a bakery
when I went to serve Mass or sing Mass at 6:00am.

After all these years, that church smells the same,
and the bakery there still, after faith
long ago left me
for younger choirboys.

My Javelin

There is a bubble of energy around me
that sometimes shows herself,
keen and bright
as a prism's refractions of my soul.

About six feet from my face,
behind, below, above,
I am surrounded in my little universe,
and her amniotic presence comes to me
once a month
or so.

I cannot summon her,
no, I must wait.

I have learned
that her appearance tests my hold
on all that my artist's ego asks of me.

This bubble,
springing like Hera from Zeus' head,
surrounds me now in glittering peace
for awhile.

Her presence around me,
depression's wet dew
not yet dry on my shoes,
I feel confident, like David,
looking at ordinary stones
formed in the primordial furnace,
Goliath's hot breath overhead.

I see that I am at the edge
of my universe:
near to where my background ends.

Yes, near to where hard efforts have
fledged me into high places
I'd not imagined.

Fledged me here
where new space/time is being created.
… just six feet away.

If, standing here
at creation's edge, I throw my javelin,
where will it go?

Ragtime

An old rag is evoked in new notes
as Bolcom's set of 22 new rags
plays in my basement studio
on Saturday afternoon.

An authentic life his.

Eubie (Blake),
Bill (Bolcom),
Rudi (Blesh),
you make me blush with love for music,
for you,
and for life
lived all the way down.

And
down here
in the basement
I wonder at it all up above me.
I wonder at those mighty in achievement
above us all, living the true.

On stage too much
we've each had some of Eden's fruit.
Yet escaping my ego's performance
through effort,
I doubt any doubt I've ever had
about leaping over it all.

And a ragtime player knows
about large strides, taking in more than
a few octaves over and over, in stride.

Don't we repeat
bad and good patterns like our music,
but mostly know
it all outside the right pulse?

And
as I think about it,
it's when I leave my own pulse behind
and outside the painful ragged
pull of time –
that's when things go badly for me.

Today though,
all is well in my ragged times.
I take my life in small beats.
Like Joplin urged us long ago
I play the rag
slowly.

If I Don't Make it Home...

Fatigue again today,
the first time in over two months.

Depression with me too, since 10:00am

BP: 105/60. Pulse: 47.

I am barely alive.

No energy for work.

Why do I need a reason to stop driving myself?
All this darkness Lifts…
eventually.

It is 2:00pm as I write.
I've made it again…
("what, John, like crossing the Rubicon")
Do I have
Kaufmann's aneurysm?
Am I just crazy?

Shaking all morning, I had four Sinemet pills.

I dream of endless rooms unfolding
into narrowing pathways on my way home to Cincinnati…
again.

I dream
of packing for the journey,
the final time.

There are lots of artifacts:
things are connected tongue and groove,
like the way spirits dig into me.

Vistas of the clean beckon.
I need to clear away sins of my past.

Faith Journey of a Catholic Child

In second grade Sr. Therese Miriam, S. C.,
told about Noah and the animals of the Ark.

> "Now, the Ark of Noah couldn't possibly have
> REALLY held two of every
> single animal, but he took every animal that he saw."

And we all thought this was reasonable,
except for Robert,
who never got to the root understanding of anything,
except for the day he wrapped his index cards
in rubber bands,
while mine all fell out of my arms that first grade afternoon.

On a seventh grade afternoon
Sr. Francis Elizabeth, S. C., told us that

> "these Bible stories are not literal matters of faith,
> but, if we choose to believe
> all 'as written' the Church will accept this, too."
> ("And Jack, you have a priestly vocation, and I want you to
> talk with my friend, Fr. Coffee, of the Holy Ghost Fathers.")

That Easter Vigil (1959) I received my conversion.
And years later, Fr. Edmund Hussey, Fr. Jesse Lonsway,
Fr. Paul Fry, and many others confirmed all this,
with no internal contradiction or conspiracy.

At my 1971 (at age 25) interview at St. Paul's, San Diego,
Fr. Jack Sanford informed me, after my very stupid opening
statement about revealed truth, that

> "too many read the scriptures with
> too little depth of consciousness."
> And that "we can be informed by God through dreams,
> tradition, teachers, and by anything else," about
> truth, immutable and eternal.

So aren't we all, at all times, sitting in the gold mine of
God's revelation?

Ordinary Gallantry

It is comforting to hear
Greek and Russian
spoken at Pete's Fruits & Vegetables
at Cedar and Holly.

Old Babushkas
squeezing beets the size of melons,
fruit in every stage of ripeness
and over-ripeness,
and the largest cabbage heads
I've ever seen are everywhere.

Last March, Pete sold me a five gallon
can of olive oil for three dollars.
It leaked a little, of course, but this was
five gallons of olive oil for $3.00!

The merchandise is part salvage,
part fresh, all very cheap.
There young families too,
speaking Greek to Pete and his son, Theo.
Behind the counter is a travel poster
for Finikouda, Greece,
a perfect Mediterranean scene and
adorned with currency from everywhere.

Now, the checkout at Pete's
is a cash operation,
with an old cash register and
scale for weighing those huge beets.

The line backs up five or six deep,
but moves very fast, with virtuoso speed
on that old cash register.

Two ahead of me, a young woman with
a little boy pack their groceries into a
large cardboard box.

It takes a long time,
and at the end of it all
she offers to pay with a credit card.

Well,
you could almost see smoke
coming out the ears of those in line.
A woman in front of me,
face round and lined
as an over-ripe Ukrainian pumpkin,
says something in Russian
needing no translation.

George, behind the counter,
goes into the back with the credit card.
He emerges after some time,
the young woman signs,
just as her boy picks up some candy.

"Let him keep it, pay me next time,"
George says *"and Theo, carry this box out to the lady's car."*

And this is an example of ordinary gallantry.

My Father's Funeral

"He called to the nurses' station, like always," she told me.
"And when I went to him he was gone."
Ninety three years and twenty three days was his time on earth.

Two bottles of Seagrams', fifteen/twenty Ibold cigars a day, give or take, has killed men, I'm told. But Dad, like an artist making it look easy, strongly smelling of the earth and more, took natural possession of things at hand,
and day by day, lived on and on, destroying demons as they'd reappear.

On the next Monday, at the nursing home, I collected my Dad's last possession, a small metal two frame picture holder with my photo at two years, and of my mother at her engagement.

Fr. W. took me to dinner that night, after I'd gone to the funeral home for a private viewing of my dad's body. He was dressed in a blue suit he'd saved for his burial as long as I can remember, and there were some cigars in his pocket which he'd left there some years ago.

Marc Glass, a decade after he inherited dad's ubiquitous presence along with his job, put a bottle of whiskey in the casket along with dad's funeral director's license. On Tuesday, visitation at 9:30am, Mass at 10:30, family and friends trickled in and told the old stories. The Gilligans, now sons and grandsons of my dad's former bosses, came through big time. They were dignified and stoical, professional, and tender in handling one of their own. The Knights of Columbus, Catholic War Vets, and Kiwanis all sent men who said prayers. Six pall bearers (five Gilligans and Marc) carried the flag-draped casket across the street to St. Lawrence. It was a powerful, moving, professional job, so important to funeral business pros.

Fr. W. gave a brief and thoughtful homily/eulogy. Jerry Schaedle solidly played the great organ, rebuilt with his own hands. There was a female singer I didn't know; and four hymns including Old 100th and Hursley, with service music typical of what is done in Catholic churches these days. About twenty attended the church funeral.

At the cemetery a military honor guard, two men in full US Navy dress, read prayers for their WW II comrade, played taps and gave me the folded flag, saluting me, eyes looking into mine about six inches away. Tucked inside the flag's folds were three empty rifle shells in lieu of a gun salute.

Six of my relatives were there, uncle Dr. Bill Tepe plus five cousins/spouses, three of whom had read during Mass. There were only six of us at the cemetery, plus Fr. W. and the funeral team, all of whom stayed to seal the burial vault.

I went back there later that afternoon and saw the grave neatly filled with red Cincinnati soil. And I remembered playing there as a boy, when the cemetery was being built, and I wondered if my hands had touched that very dirt long ago.

My dad occupies what had been the last remaining grave on the family plot, six buried there in all now. My mother (Martha), aunts Alice and Cathyrne ("your dad would give away his ass") Byrne, and my maternal grandparents, Joseph Sylvester ("Deutches Reich") Byrne, and his wife Martha Tyighe Byrne. The afternoon was hot and humid.

Alone there, I said my last prayers and headed for the airport, and to my home with Bess.

Choir Rehearsal
An old Choirmaster Looks Back

I've led church choirs
since I was 15 years old,
and reflecting now,
some 50 years later,
little has changed.

Choir rehearsal begins
as I am approached by a singer
as if marching to war:

> "it seems like you don't care if I come to
> rehearsal or not because you didn't call
> me after I missed last week.
>
> My heels are so small that my shoes slip
> off of my feet. I wish we didn't have to
> wear those shoes to church."

Into a Lenten chorale by Bach,
someone, failing at a fermata:

> "John, I can't follow your conducting."
>
> "Right," I say,
> "you're absolutely right, you can't."

Moving on, someone else opines that

> "it might be helpful if the Altos
> put the 'd' sound on the eighth rest."

Well, now.

I wonder about many things
as the music flows on

> (Why don't I just
> get by with blatant posturing
> about the irrelevant
> and then, get credit
> for being a *"stickler for details"?*)

And will I, in a minute or so,
when someone raises some logistical
question that doesn't need answering
for another month,
or asks when break will start,
with God's help,
will I be able to evade sarcasm?

A half-baked Socratic dialogue
ensues into my thoughts:
*And now, Glaucon,
let us assume that we, and many others
are in a boat, floating in water.*

*And let us further assume that we see
many turds afloat.
And suppose someone in the boat
observes this and announces:
"you know, I see a turd floating
in the water; I shall do something about
that turd."*

*Now, Glaucon, since the turd works no
evil on us, but floats away in due course;
is this not a case of the perfect becoming
an enemy of the good?)*

I leave my friends in the boat,
as music in the full flow of glory,
awakes.

With my cue,
"*spirito*" on the next downbeat,
someone sings   fff
"Alleluia!"
It rhymes perfectly with
"Al Léluja."
Now this is time for humor.

I stop, check my timing

"Oh yes, Al Léluja, voco angelico, piu
grasso. I remember when he sang the
National Anthem every year at Yankee
Stadium."

My choir laughs at another bad joke,
I store away the turd dialogue,
and I again find healing release,
through common talk,
in the deep well of God's grace.

Pondering My Finitude at 70

As I near my 70th birthday, my finitude comes into thoughts, keenly and more often. My parents, grandparents and aunts are all buried at St. Joseph Cemetery.

And whenever I travel to Cincinnati,
I go to the gravesite to pray.

About 60 years ago, St. Joseph's was under construction. Land was being cleared,
planted, readied for the dead.

My friend, Charles, and I played there
during one particular summer of St. Joseph's building. There was one very large mound of red Cincinnati clay dirt into which we dug a cave of sorts. When I think of it now, it's a wonder it didn't bury us there in the cemetery one sunny afternoon.

We were there day after day, digging into imagined secrecy and mystery, like esoteric initiates. There at our cave one day I heard a distant crack far off to the south.

An instant later a high whirring sound sped by my right ear.

The sound lasted about a second.
Then, another crack and the same whirring sound again.

Innocent of such things, it was years later that I realized someone had shot at us, and just missed.

I actually heard the bullets passing probably inches from my head. And I think now just how close my finitude was then to the empty family grave site.

Genesis 22:13

And Abraham lifted up his eyes
They were before fixed upon his son lying upon the altar, and
intent upon that part he was going to thrust his knife into;
but hearing a voice from heaven above him, he lifted up his
eyes thitherward:

There is always, somewhere, a ram in the bushes.
It is what we are that leads us to the ram.

The ram is the vehicle that has been ignored but fed.
Maybe it is Dharma, or the Grail castle.

All knowing depends on the ram.

"… and they didn't call it a 'church key' for nothing, Cosmo."

The ram must be burned up for it to be resurrected.

Wagner knew this when he wrote
Brünhilda's immolation scene.

Continuing education teaching could show a straight path
to the ram in bushes.

Sacrifice of the ram leaves the sacred residue. This is the
true prima material of the alchemists.

Alphabetical Index

A
A Bird Spoke to Me Last Night 36
Afraid at Night 56
A Monk of the Abbey 75
Ancient Warriors' Song 53
An Idea of Winter 27
Augean Stables 31
Auntie 65

B
Bang 7

C
Cardiac Catheterization 24
Choir Rehearsal 86
Christmas Delivery 2
The Chronicle of Change 42
Claude's Software of the Soul 46
Committee Meeting 57
Composers' Panel 73

D
Dream Song for Uncle Bill Kuzma 52

E
Ecclesiad 77
"Eskimo Pies"™ 34

F
Faith Journey of a Catholic Child 81
Family 39
Faust's Seeker 59
The Fire of Prometheus 1
The Fly 69
Friday Afternoon at the Bank 8
From Cosmo 74

G
Genesis 22:13 89

H
Hard 72
Heaven and Earth in Little Space 14

I
If I Don't Make it Home… 80

J
Jack Mad with Music 55
Jack's Catenary Curve 67
Ιεροσόλυμα 68
Jimmy's News 5
Jungian Dream 35

L
Leyden & Colfax 6

M

Mentorship...21
The Mirror...61
Moth...16
My Father's Funeral 84
My Heart Dances Her Way – CardioDance 1 & 2 40
My Javelin...78
My Real Destination 15
My Room..38

O

One Heck of a Dog..20
Ordinary Gallantry...82
Organ Music at Cincinnati's "Old Odeon" 71

P

Pate of Foie Gras..63
Pondering My Finitude at 70 88
Prostate Trouble 50
Purity..9
Pygmies..47

R

Ragtime..79
Rolodex™...76

S

The Sage of Kearney Street 19
Scents...64
Snowy Last Night 29
Solitude and Friendship....................................70
Sonnet of Confession 23
Souls on the Stable Road...................................26
Spider in the Cold...28
Stravinsky's Sacre du Printemps at 100 37
Supermarket 10
Supermarket - Cigar Head...................................13
Surfaces...45

T

The Thing Itself I'll Be 58
Thoughts on a Snowy Night..................................22
Thoughts Rambling on Monday Night 43
Transition to Final Things.................................44

U

Ubiquitous Genius..62
Unbearable Nostalgia.......................................54
Upon Waking During Deep Brain Stimulation Surgery 32

W

What Do We Have, Really?...................................30
What Isn't Obvious at the Buffalo Grill....................48
"Would you like to sign this petition?"....................12